D1454832

The Multicultural Campus

Dedications

Dedicated to my homies
Mae, Louis, and Elizabeth
from whom I learned appreciation
for human diversity

L. A. Castenell, Jr.

Dedicated to the "old gang" (my classmates) of
Malabar Elementary School
Belvedere Junior High School
Roosevelt High School
of East L.A.
from whom I learned, early in life, the true value
of diversity and multiculturalism

L. A. Valverde

The Multicultural Campus

Strategies for Transforming Higher Education

Leonard A. Valverde
Louis A. Castenell, Jr.
Editors

ALTAMIRA
PRESS

A Division of Sage Publications, Inc.
Walnut Creek ■ London ■ New Delhi

/ 99&

For information address:

AltaMira Press
A Division of Sage Publications, Inc.
1630 North Main Street, Suite 367
Walnut Creek, California 94596 USA
explore@altamira.sagepub.com

Sage Publications, Ltd.
6 Bonhill Street
London, EC2A 4PU United Kingdom

Sage Publications India Pvt. Ltd.
M-32 Market
Greater Kailash I
New Delhi 100 048 India

PRINTED IN THE UNITED STATES OF AMERICA

Library of Congress Cataloging-in-Publication Data

The Multicultural Campus: Strategies for Transforming Higher Education / edited by Leonard A. Valverde and Louis A. Castenell.
    p.   cm.
    Includes bibliographical references and index.
    ISBN 0–7619–9165–4 (cloth). —0–7619–9166–2 (pbk.).
    1. Minorities—Education (Higher)—United States. 2. African Americans—Education (Higher). 3. Asian Americans—Education (Higher). 4. Hispanic Americans—Education (Higher). 5. Multicultural education—United States. I. Valverde, Leonard A. II. Castenell, Louis Anthony, 1947–
LC3727.M83 1998
378.1'9829—DC21   97–4593
                                                                       CIP
98   99   00   01   02   03   9   8   7   6   5   4   3   2   1

Editorial Management: Kathleen Paparchontis
Editorial Production: Carole Bernard, ECS
Cover Design: Eric Akeson

Contents

Foreword

Leonard A. Valverde and Louis A. Castenell, Jr. have put together a timely book that focuses needed attention on a topic of great moment—the need to transform colleges and universities of this country in ways that will enable them to serve more effectively the needs of the different kinds of students coming to their campuses now and in the new millennium. In my opinion, nothing is more urgent, more pressing, for higher education leaders than to address "diversity issues" on our respective campuses.

In prior years, this set of issues was variously identified as race relations concerns, or the interethnic, interracial problem, or multiculturalism, or simply affirmative action concerns. Whatever the label, the reality being addressed was simply what to do about the increased presence of people of color on U.S. college campuses. How and to what extent should colleges and universities change to cope with these new, always highly visible, university dwellers? Of late, this issue has beome a controversial matter for mostly the wrong reasons, and that is what Valverde and Castenell and the other authors address head-on.

This book is important because it impels us to refocus attention on this "burning issue of our day," which many have been trying to relegate to the back burner recently. For, in my opinion, too many of our important leaders today truly believe that the "matter of race" has been settled and that we must now move on to more important things. Nothing could be further from the truth. Because whether one chooses to believe otherwise or not, the problem of race and ethnicity in America remains a serious matter of unfinished business. And, at the core of this continuing dilemma, is the pressing need to push more strongly than ever to ensure the full participation of the different racial and ethnic groups that make up the mosaic of our society.

Through their shaping and preparatory efforts, the colleges and universities of America continue to be the gatekeepers that determine who our future leaders will be. This makes it imperative that all these institutions must change, must be pushed, if need be, to move in the right direction and in the right ways. That is what Valverde and Castenell and the authors of the different chapters of this book are compelling those of us in academe to face up to.

Every author in this book brings an important analytical perspective to this set of issues, and every one has their own ideas for reform and change. Each one presents importantly different ways to look at the complexities involved in improving the ways that institutions of higher education respond to the increased presence of students, faculty, and staff of color.

Collectively, the authors delve with keen insight into how institutions are dealing with the need to increase the presence of minorities on campus and why minorities continue to be grossly underrepresented in faculty and administrative leadership positions. It is these insights and differences in perspectives that lend importance to this book.

Current anti-affirmative action measures, immigrant bashing, nativistic pronouncements, and public expressions of alarm about the growing numbers of "predominantly minority, low-achieving public schools" together deliver a rather troublesome message about the perceived state of conditions in America that should concern us all. They add urgency to the need for positive leadership to move us to higher ground. But this will not be possible unless we first begin to understand better the nature of our problems. Higher education leaders must be in the forefront in bringing about the requisite changes, but first they must have a clear understanding of the issues discussed in this book. Valverde, Castenell, and company, with their descriptive analyses of the real-world faced by minorities on our campuses, provide the truly interested with a sound way to get beyond what newspapers report.

Tomas A. Arciniega, President
California State University, Bakersfield

Preface

This collection of writings is addressed to help individuals create higher education campuses that have pluralistic climates—climates that not only allow culturally diverse individuals and groups to feel comfortable but that promote multicultural environments.

The approach taken is simple. Dr. Castenell and I first identified people of color who held either administrative, faculty, or student positions within the university. We asked the senior academics in administrative roles to list strategies they have used to forge a multicultural environment. Next, we requested the junior academics to describe strategies they had observed that supported cultural pluralism on campuses. Finally, we invited a student to write about strategies he had noted on campuses that recognized his cultural values and norms. This assignment required considerable reflection and analysis from all the participants and the ability to express their suggestions in meaningful ways to a large audience. We are delighted with their responses.

Although each author worked independently, surprisingly we discovered common strategies among the chapters. The contributors identified similar strategies in part because of the following commonalities: (1) People of color experience similar struggles, (2) People of color benefit from the same nationally created "opportunities," (3) Since people of color experience similar problem situations, they forge like responses, and (4) Lastly, the psychological profile of people of color is consistent within ethnic or racial subgroups and is divergent from the so-called dominant white culture and from the institutional customs and practices found on higher education campuses.

One last observation requires highlighting for the reader. While reading the incoming manuscripts, we noticed that strategies were not just targeted toward institutional change. Of necessity, the authors also focused on strengthening the affected ethnic or racial minority groups or individuals.

Because historically the forces at work have damaged the collective ego of generations of these groups, strategies were mandatory to shore up the individual belief in self. In fact, we, as editors, would be remiss if we failed to acknowledge this human characteristic. For what it reveals is the valiant behavior by these authors and other nonidentified pioneers working to create a more democratic society. These courageous men and women struggled to develop both a strong sense of self-efficacy and a conceptual framework that favored multiculturalism.

PART I

Introduction and Overview

LOUIS A. CASTENELL, JR. ■

Introduction

Dominant cultures shape the larger contexts and substance of all learning in society. Higher education is no exception. As emerging cultures clash with dominant ones, an evolutionary process takes place. This is nowhere more apparent in U.S. higher education than in its struggle with excellence, accountability, and diversity. A common way that institutions of higher education attempt to manage these tensions is by promoting successful people of color. This text will illuminate select experiences and ideas of successful leaders of color. The purpose of these articles is to provide insight into the challenges and rewards these individuals experienced. A clear understanding of how culture and higher education relate to one another will help frame subsequent discussions in this volume.

The creation of Harvard College in 1636 was the beginning of higher education in the United States. Harvard and other colonial colleges borrowed much of their administrative, organizational, and curricular structures from medieval universities (Gutek, 1986). Gutek makes two critical points. One, enrollment in colonial colleges came primarily from the economically favored and socially prominent classes. Two, there continues to be significant interaction between transplanted European concepts and higher education in the United States. Colon (1991) remarks that "colleges and universities, though they have their own unique cultural identities, are inclined to transmit the dominant societal culture" (p. 72). Luz Reyes and Halcon (1991) argue that "the academy mirrors the same attitudes and generalities about cultural/racial differences that plague the larger society" (p. 171). Although universities are thought to be more liberal than the general population in the United States, university administrators, especially their faculty, are rather conservative on matters relating to change in the university (Altbach, 1991). Thus, the academy is struggling with many of today's challenges, most notably what constitutes curricula, diversity, and accountability issues.

Kennedy (1995) begins the discussion by reminding us that there is a high level of public disaffection about what our colleges and universities are doing. He points to the broad and negative news coverage of everything from racial incidents and intercollegiate athletic scandals to sexual harassment and scientific fraud. Furthermore, this disaffection increases the level of anxiety within the institutions. Recently, a 1989 survey of 150 American college and university presidents representing all 50 states and all segments of American higher education, governors of the 50 states, and 50 other higher education leaders identified seven critical issues (Gilley, 1991). The first three were concerned with minority participation in higher education and finance. For the purpose of this volume, we shall limit our discussion to their first issue: minority participation in the academy.

There are many good reasons why colleges and universities are concerned about the relatively small number of minorities on campus. Altbach argues that "[d]ue in part to legal requirements from the federal government and, in the case of public universities, to political pressures from state governments, and in part from an institutional sense of responsibility and an understanding of the changing demographics of American life, many colleges and universities have tried to increase minority representation on campus" (1991, p. 14).

Justiz, Wilson, and Bjork (1994) further argue that increasing minorities is a critical aspect of changing institutional culture and climate; however, Wong (1991) reminds us that those groups—most notably African

Americans, Hispanic Americans, and Asian Americans—present a new cultural diversity that more directly challenges a traditional culture of academe, "a culture shaped by Anglo European influences" (p. 53). These new groups resist assimilation and have argued for the right to contribute to the redefining of academic tradition based on their insights and experience. A brief overview of these three major minority groups will shed more light on this expanding debate.

African Americans

African Americans constitute 12.3% of the population but only 8.7 percent of college enrollment and 5.7% of college graduates (Justiz et al., 1994). These authors pointed out that 42% of all African American students were enrolled in two-year institutions. Unfortunately, research indicates that most students who begin in two-year colleges do not complete the baccalaureate degree (Altbach & Lomotey, 1991). In 1991, only 3.8% of doctoral degrees in the United States were awarded to African Americans (Payne, 1994). As with all other degrees, the small recent gains of African Americans are still a major problem, especially when we consider that African Americans compose only 2% of the faculty (Gilley, 1991).

The above statistics do not tell the full story. Altbach (1991) draws our attention to the fact that there are fewer African Americans in the high-prestige sector of American higher education than in all other institutions of higher education. "Their numbers tend to be concentrated in less selective public colleges, in community colleges, and of course in the traditionally black institutions" (p. 9). Regardless of where African American professionals are, they face unique challenges. Since 1985, the majority of African American faculty are employed in nonhistorically Black colleges and universities (Jackson, 1991). Also, since 1987 African American students were more likely to graduate from predominately white colleges than from historically Black colleges and universities (HBCU). Jackson's research indicates these students are less prone to pursue a career in the academic world. He states that the data suggest that African American students enrolled in predominately white institutions "average higher attrition rates, greater states of alienation, and perhaps most significantly, less satisfactory relationships with faculty" (p. 139). By contrast, African American students in HBCU show evidence of greater retention and academic gains plus higher attainment aspirations.

The small gains in college graduates, coupled with a relatively small number of graduate students in the pipeline, make for a fragile future for African Americans.

Hispanic Americans

Hispanics are made up of many Spanish-speaking groups. According to the U.S. Bureau of the Census, the largest group is of Mexican origin (64%). The next largest group is comprised of individuals from Central and South America (14%), then, in smaller numbers, there are individuals from Puerto Rico (10.6%), Cuba (4.7%), and other areas (7%). Each group is unique and complex. Nonetheless, national databases frequently include non-American Hispanics into their calculations. This makes it difficult to assess participation of Hispanic Americans, especially in education. Despite this flaw, the number of Hispanics in higher education remains low relative to their population.

Hispanics constitute 8.1% of the population but only 4.7% of higher education enrollment and 2.7% of graduates (Carrasquillo, 1991). The majority of Hispanic students are in community colleges; however, Solmon and Wingard (1991) note that Hispanics are most likely to begin their college careers in public two-year colleges. This is especially troubling as they point out that less than 10% of community college students transfer to four-year colleges or universities.

Luz Reyes and Halcon (1991) report that only 2% of all doctoral degrees are awarded to Hispanics. Furthermore, Hispanic faculty in four-year institutions make up about 2% of the total faculty. And these writers draw our attention to the fact that even this small number is often relegated to ethnically oriented programs such as ethnic studies, Spanish departments, and student support services. In 1993, only 2.6% of the presidents of the 3,611 U.S. colleges and universities were Hispanics. Unfortunately, little is known about the professional training, social origins, and career mobility of Hispanic higher education administrators (Santos & Rigual, 1994).

The current status of Hispanics in higher education in the United States remains precarious. Despite the recent surge in immigration, projected higher birth rates, and larger number of children in their family units, recent attacks on affirmative action and immigration policies suggest that the percent of Hispanics seeking college degrees will continue to plummet in coming years.

Asian Americans

The Asian American population is projected to grow to nearly 10 million by 2000. They comprise 4% of the total U.S. population (Suzuki, 1994). Suzuki reports that between 1982 and 1991, Asian American enrollments in higher education increased by 81% and constituted 4.4% of the total enrollment. By the year 2000, they will constitute 10% of all students. Although the majority of Asian Americans attend four-year colleges or universities, 41% attend community colleges (Gilley, 1991). Between 1988–89 to 1992–93, there was a modest increase of about 4% of earned degrees by Asian Americans (Borden, 1996). However, Asian Americans showed signs of leveling off in all categories except first professional degrees.

Similar to Hispanics, all 29 Asian groups are aggregated into one category, thus obscuring unique group differences, according to Suzuki (1994). For instance, he notes that "most academic institutions do not desegregate data on Asian Americans" (p. 265). This practice conceals substantial group differences such as high success of Japanese and Chinese and economic and academic challenges of newer groups from Southeast Asia.

The challenges facing Asian Americans remain strong. Despite their apparent success in higher education, there is strong evidence that current practices discriminate against Asian Americans. Solmon and Wingard (1991) report that the number of doctorates awarded to Asians who are permanent residents in the United States, especially Asians studying on temporary visas, far exceeds those awarded to Asian Americans.

As American colleges and universities are expected to take the lead in addressing many of our societal problems, House (1994) reminds us that higher education has led a charmed life in late twentieth-century America; but this protected status is unlikely to continue. The subsequent chapters provide examples of how people of color have succeeded despite the odds. It is hoped that their personal lessons, experiences, and views will create a more favorable climate to correct practices and ideas that contribute to the underrepresentation of academic leaders of color.

REFERENCES

Altbach, P. G. (1991). The racial dilemma in American higher education. In P. G. Altbach & K. Lomotey (Eds.), *The racial crisis in American higher education* (pp. 3–17). Albany: State University of New York Press. Albany: State University of New York Press.

Altbach, P. G., & Lomotey, K. (Eds.). (1991). *The racial crisis in American higher education.* Albany: State University of New York Press.

Borden, V. (1996). Five-year trends in minority degree production. *Black Issues in Higher Education, 13*(7), 34–71.

Carrasquillo, A. (1991). *Hispanic children and youth in the United States.* New York: Garland Press.

Colon, A. (1991). Race relations on campus. In P. G. Altbach & K. Lomotey (Eds.), *The racial crisis in American higher education* (pp. 69–88). Albany: State University of New York Press.

Gilley, J. W. (1991). *Thinking about American higher education.* New York: Macmillan.

Gutek, G. L. (1986). *Education in the United States.* Englewood Cliffs, NJ: Prentice-Hall.

House, E. R. (1994). Policy and productivity in higher education. *Educational Researcher, 23*(5), 27–32.

Jackson, K. W. (1991). Black faculty in academia. In P. G. Altbach & K. Lomotey (Eds.), *The racial crisis in American higher education* (pp. 135–148). Albany: State University of New York Press.

Justiz, M., Wilson, R., & Bjork, L. (1994). *Minorities in higher education.* Phoenix: Oryx Press.

Kennedy, D. (1995). Another century's end, another revolution for higher education. *Change, 27*(3), 8–15.

Payne, N. J. (1994). Maintaining the competitive tradition. In M. Justiz, R. Wilson, & L. Bjork (Eds.), *Minorities in higher education* (pp. 210–238). Phoenix: Oryx Press.

Luz Reyes, M. de la, & Halcon, J. J. (1991). Practices of the academy: Barriers to access for Chicano academics. In P. G. Altbach & K. Lomotey (Eds.), *The racial crisis in American higher education* (pp. 167–186). Albany: State University of New York Press.

Santos, A. de los, & Rigual, A. (1994). *Progress of Hispanics in American higher education.* In M. Justiz, R. Wilson, & L. Bjork (Eds.), *Minorities in higher education* (pp. 173–194). Phoenix: Oryx Press.

Solmon, L. C., & Wingard, T. L. (1991). The changing demographics: Problems and opportunities. In P. G. Altbach and K. Lomotey (Eds.), *The racial crisis in American higher education* (pp. 19–42). Albany: State University of New York Press.

Suzuki, B. H. (1994). Higher education issues in the Asian American community. In M. Justiz, R. Wilson, & L. Bjork (Eds.). *Minorities in higher education* (pp. 258–285). Phoenix, Oryx Press.

Wong, F. (1991). Diversity and community: Right objectives and wrong arguments. *Change, 23*(4), 48–54.

LEONARD A. VALVERDE ■

One

Future Strategies and Actions:
Creating Multicultural
Higher Education Campuses

Using the last 35 years (since 1963) to frame the discussion of the gradual inclusion of multiculturalism in higher education institutions and to measure the progress of diversifying postsecondary campuses, reported statistics reveal an up-and-down trend (Carter & Wilson, 1992). Although the early strategies have varied, the primary target has been greater inclusion of minorities. More specifically, the various strategies have focused primarily on increasing the number of students of color. During these three and a half decades, the overall picture reveals that the majority of traditionally underrepresented groups have been enrolled in community colleges, fewer in four-year public universities than in community colleges, and fewest in major research universities (Olivas, 1986).

Three other trends appear when one examines the participation level of people of color in higher education. (1) The retention rates become worse as racial or ethnic minority groups move from undergraduate degrees to advanced degrees (for example, more associate of arts degrees are awarded than baccalaureate degrees, fewer master's degrees than bachelor of arts or bachelor of science degrees, and minimal doctorates and terminal degrees). (2) Participation in higher education of minorities is not proportional to either their population or to their public elementary and secondary school enrollment. (3) A look at the data shows a higher education that is segregated situationally, that is, historically Black institutions and less financially supported institutions (for example, City University of New York compared to State University of New York or California State University campuses compared to University of California campuses) typically have the greatest number of students of color.

When examining the general enrollment and graduation rates by decade, starting with the 1960s, the trend line slopes upward during the sixties, continues upward in the seventies, levels off during the eighties, and then decreases during the last decade of the twentieth century. The decrease of students of color is troubling, given that the downward trend of participation comes at the same time that students of color are increasing in high-school graduation and their SAT/ACT scores are increasing as well (Evangelauf, 1988; Manzo, 1993; Watkins, 1988).

The second major target for the greater access strategy has been the faculty ranks. The same profile materializes for minority faculty as described for students of color. That is, more minority faculty are found in the community colleges, fewer in four-year universities, and fewest in research universities. Within the university system, most minority faculty are teaching at the undergraduate level and are found primarily in the humanities and social sciences, with the fewest in the sciences and professional schools, with the exception of colleges of education.

The third target of the greater access strategy has been focused on administrative positions, such as department chairs, college deans, vice presidents, and presidents. Again, the profile of success for these influential positions is the same as described for student and faculty participation. Similarly, administrators of color are mostly in student service roles instead of in academic positions, limited primarily to positions with titles of assistant or associate, and, during the sixties, most of these positions were funded through external sources or soft money. Thus, many individuals who entered higher education institutions did so through nontraditional means and, therefore, were seen as less qualified, not mainstream in the organizational structure of the campus, and temporary instead of permanent (Blackwell, 1983).

It is not until the late seventies that the entry and promotion of faculty and administrators of color shifted from the mostly nontraditional approach to the mostly regular means of employment and upward mobility into administration. Even with this shift to a regular route of access, there is still a stereotype that faculty and administrators of color are not as competitive or qualified (that is, incentives have to be provided by the administration or regents to faculty units in order to stimulate the hiring of minority faculty. Similarly, many minority administrators are selected to hold high-ranking positions, typically after some form of public pressure is applied.

A Shift in Strategy:
From Access to Changing the Campus

During the mid-1980s, goals shifted from a press for access to a desire for meaningful participation within campuses of higher education. Just as there was a natural evolution of the Civil Rights Movement from a struggle to end segregation to a fight to establish integration, so, too, there was a natural shift from increasing the numbers of minority group members on campuses to changing the campuses so that they were more accommodating to minority group members. That is, the goal became to change a traditionally homogeneous white institution into one that was heterogeneous or at least less racist. Hence, as the goal changed, so, too, did the strategies.

The evolved or newer strategies served two goals: (1) to combat racist policies and practices vested in campuses; and (2) to forge campuses that included traits and events that reflected a pluralistic society. As a result of these two goals, numerous scholars and individuals who had experienced merely inclusion on monocultural campuses developed strategies that would expose the realities of such higher education campuses. One such strategy was identifying and revealing negative policies and adverse practices. For example, problems and issues of concern that produced conflict between white students and students of color and between white faculty and faculty/administrators of color were written about and/or presented at public forums. In addition, special committees and/or task forces were assembled and charged to study these identified problems; reports were generated with recommendations as to how to stop the problem; and discussion and dissemination occurred.

The second goal led to another set of strategies—that of creating a climate on campuses that would help traditionally excluded populations feel more comfortable and be more successful (that is, students would complete their program of study so as to graduate, or faculty would be successful in the tenure and promotion process). This second set of strategies is discussed in the following chapters. Strategies to create multicultural campuses are, for the most part, internally (within campuses) conceived and controlled. However, at the beginning of the goal shift (from access to campus modification), the strategies were driven by incentives provided mostly by external funding sources (for example, federal agencies or private foundations). In general, administrators and faculty are motivated to put in place strategies that will accommodate a diverse student body because government leaders, private influences, regents, or system chancellors have declared such activities a priority.

Current and Future Influential Dynamics

The shift from accessing higher education institutions to modifying the environment of higher education campuses is depicted in Diagram 1. Simplistically, Diagram 1 visualizes the five sequential stages a campus undergoes.

DIAGRAM 1
Stages of Multiculturing a Campus

Stages	One	Two	Three	Four	Five
Type	Monocultural campus	Ethnocentric campus	Accommodating campus	Transitional campus	Transformed campus
Characteristic	Devoid of minority traits	Dominant white culture, which admits minority	Personnel and policies modified to accommodate people of color	Limited pluralism	Multicultural in all aspects

If one examines the fourth stage in Diagram 1, then the logic of why greater access by any previously excluded group of persons ultimately leads to altering the environment becomes apparent. By plotting the participation and access of higher education campuses by ethnic/racial persons of color on a two-dimensional axis, the transformation is easy to understand. Please refer to Diagram 2 below. If the vertical axis, labeled *participation*, represents the level of influence one has on the environment as a result of involvement with various elements of the campus, and if the horizontal axis,

DIAGRAM 2
Group Capacity to Transform Campus

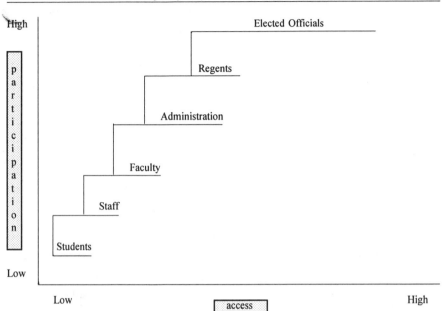

labeled *access*, represents the amount of time one spends on the campus, then the ability or potential to create change on campuses can be explained.

The obvious should be stated. Since American campuses of higher education are in the early stages of transformation, most campuses have undergone a limited degree of change—from being monocultural campuses to having a multicultural environment. Clearly, infusion of cultural pluralism has occurred, but few campuses are fully multicultural. Even in those campuses that embraced cultural diversity early through student enrollments and that continue to work at diversifying their campuses, there remains an inequity of multiculturalism in substance and a lack of parity in value of the concept.

For example, students have potential to cause changes but not as much as staff since students are a transient population, matriculating through the campus over a prescribed (usually short) period of time, whereas staff are more long term in their employment. On the vertical axis, staff have more control over resources than students and, therefore, their participation level is higher than students. Similarly, faculty have more power to cause change than staff because faculty have longer employment (tenure) and more participation due to collegial process than staff.

Since focus of access by people of color into American higher education institutions resulted from societal forces begun by the Civil Rights Movement during the early 1960s, the progress, or lack thereof, has been dependent on societal dynamics. Therefore, when considering strategic ways to accomplish the goal of access, or any other goal such as creating greater participation by persons of color in higher education, societal influences need to be factored in.

In the mid-1990s, there are more negative than positive forces in play, although some of the initial positive forces may continue. The main negative force working against early initiatives is the philosophy of conservatism. For the first time in 40 years, Congress has changed from being an institution controlled by the Democrats (perceived to be liberal) to one with a Republican majority (more conservative). Far–right-wing groups such as various militias have surfaced. The Christian Coalition is more politically active, particularly in local school board elections. All of these forces have targeted civil rights legislation. At the center of the challenges is affirmative action, the core of equal opportunity. Affirmative action legislation, for example, California's Proposition 209, and policies are under attack by way of political debate and, more seriously, by litigation.

Another major negative force at work is the economic variable; the cost of getting a higher education degree has risen steadily. Concurrently, state legislatures have been reducing their support of state higher education institutions. As is typical, middle-class families and first-time college goers, that is, the poor and people of color, are hit the hardest.

Although the politics are getting worse and economics are making it more difficult for people of color to access higher education institutions, some forces are working in their favor. Specifically and most importantly, the demographic trend of increasing numbers of people of color will force higher education campuses to develop proactive strategies to create multicultural campuses. People of color are increasing in numbers because of various factors: (1) higher birth rates; (2) larger average family size for people of color than for whites; (3) immigration from Latin American, African, and Asian countries is higher than from European countries; and (4) longevity is increasing more for people of color than for whites (U.S. Bureau of the Census, 1990a). The U.S. Bureau of the Census (1990b) projects that by 2050 the population of the United States will be a majority of "minorities."

In addition to greater numbers, and while the political forces ebb and flow, it is important to note that affirmative action policies and laws are withstanding legal challenges. For example, California's Proposition 187 is on hold, and Arizona's English Only challenge has been unsuccessful in that state's Supreme Court. The overall political prediction is favorable for the people of color. The reasoning behind this positive prediction is simple: As "minority" population numbers increase and as these subgroups register to vote and exercise their voting rights, people of color will increase their societal power which will likely permit a better set of circumstances across the board, including higher education participation.

The Unfinished Agenda Continued

During the decades since the 1960s, we have learned much about what needs to take place if colleges and universities are to recruit, enroll, and graduate a larger number of students of color, as well as hire and promote faculty and increase the number of minority-group persons in leadership positions. While the majority of past strategies were aimed at access, in the next 20 years there will probably have to be a shift in focus aimed at transforming higher education campuses into multicultural environments. In other words, future strategies will have two parallel targets: One will be to continue to increase access and the other will be to emphasize the transformation process. It will be necessary to have dual targets because campuses will not be transformed without a sustained multicultural population nor will it be possible to maintain a pluralistic campus without replenishing its student body, faculty, and administration. Research literature tells us that it takes approximately 50 years for an innovation to be institutionalized in an education agency (Sergiovanni & Starratt, 1971).

Although the access agenda has had mixed success, its unevenness is due more to a lessening of commitment and political trends than to ill-conceived strategies. Much is known about access-type strategies, largely due to the emphasis on accountability, used by educational institutions. Most of the early strategies created to harvest larger numbers of minority persons into higher education were evaluated at the request of the funding source or the governing board. Consequently, with each new initiative in countless campuses across the country, an annual report was written. Lately, a new type of evaluation on access strategies has emerged—evaluations that are comprehensive in factor analysis, larger in scope, incorporate multiple campus efforts instead of just one campus, etc. (Hurtado, Figueroa, & Garcia, 1996). The large information base about access strategies along with these new aggregate studies should be of great help in devising new strategies for transforming higher education campuses.

Identification of New Strategies and Actions

Since a higher education campus consists of many different components, strategies to change the character and make-up of the campus must also use different approaches. For example, colleges or universities have a governance component, an administration arm, approved curricula, an outreach or service responsibility, a facilities operation, and so on. However, given that the primary purpose of an educational institution is to share a knowledge base in an organized fashion with individuals called students, it is wise to concentrate on the development of new strategies that focus on the primary purpose: academics. Therefore, what follows is an attempt to discuss a selected band of strategies that will alter the campus academic environment of the future. This attempt is skeletal and should not be considered all inclusive, detailed, or elaborate.

With the above as a framework to target our new strategies, strategies that will likely produce the most outcome are those aimed at: (1) the governance or policy level; (2) the executive or procedural level; and (3) the faculty and curricula level.

At the *governance or policy level*, dual-purpose strategies will be needed. For example, efforts and activities that influence the appointment process of regents will need to be used. The appointment process is still in the political arena. It is vital to establish relations with elected officials such as state representatives, congressional members, and city- and county-elected persons. There needs to be much activity and involvement with significant influential people on a wide range of social and public issues. By involvement, we mean a working relationship takes place that will be useful when trying to get adequate representation on the governing board of the college or university.

Furthermore, policy that has impact on public institutions of higher education is not immune to social involvement and thinking. Again, strategies used to influence the political process must be emphasized and practiced with more intensity and frequency. A good illustration is affirmative action. The question of affirmative action's continuation and definition is subject to open comment at the board of regents level, and therefore open to the public debate process.

At the *executive and procedural level*, the access strategies are still very much needed. Every organization has key roles or power positions. Clearly, system chancellors, campus presidents, or college deans are such critical roles. More people of color need to occupy these power positions through the customary ways in order to be "validated" in the minds of the campus community. But greater numbers of persons in these positions are insufficient to change the body of the campus. When new leaders, whether people of color or not, access these crucial positions they will have to practice a transformational style of leadership. Central to the belief system of these new leaders will have to be the appreciation that they are agents for change. Since universities and colleges are conservative by nature, they are resistant to change. The institutions see themselves more as preserving the past than as preparing people for the future. Therefore, if higher education campuses are to help advance society, leaders of higher education will have to be ignitors of change.

But, in addition to igniting change, the new leaders of higher education campuses will have to be cultural agents. Presidents and chancellors will have to appreciate and understand a variety of cultures. Since most people of color are knowledgeable about two cultures—their native culture and that of white America—they are typically more qualified to fulfill the cultural agent responsibility than their white counterparts. And, since no one individual can adequately be multicultural, the executive team of the campus should be ethnically and culturally diverse. When a multiplicity of views is represented at the executive cabinet, then practices and different perspectives more accommodating to a multicultural student body are more likely to emerge.

At the *faculty and curricula level*, the strategy probably needs to be along the lines described above, cultural and change agent, but with a twist. In Chapter 6 Professor Contreras refers to the strategy as "leading from the margins." He argues, in essence, that as many faculty of color are considered by their colleagues as marginal because they are of a lower status, that is, nontenure track or junior faculty and not in faculty positions with influence (for example, graduate adviser, program head, faculty senator, etc.), they must exercise influence in atypical ways. There are multiple leverage points that faculty of color can devise to lead from the margins. For example, they can insert new curricula into the existing courses they have been assigned to teach. They can promote new courses with new curricula. They can recruit students of color into the program of study. They can secure external funding to start a new project, which, in turn, brings in new students, faculty, and/or staff, even if on a temporary basis; alters the curriculum; and can generate new research. Faculty of color can excel in teaching, in research, or in community service and in so doing can build up a following, a support base that empowers them when they speak or which produces the perception that they command respect.

Connecting the New Strategies

Education is a labor-intensive human enterprise. The human dimension has the most influence on any campus and the most lasting power. For these reasons, three similar strategies must also be activated besides the three described above. These three strategies can be termed connecting strategies. The first of these connecting strategies is *mentoring*. Each higher level must mentor the level below it. That is, members of the governing board should mentor chancellors and presidents. Presidents, in turn, need to mentor deans, deans to mentor department chairs, senior faculty to mentor junior faculty, and faculty to mentor students (Blackwell, 1989). Remember, mentoring is an unofficial practice that takes place in the academy. The American academy is patterned after the European model, which is founded on the apprentice system.

The second connecting strategy is *networking*. Where the strategy of mentorship is mostly vertical and based on developing a close relationship governed by a one-way status—that is, top down—the concept of networking is more than vertical, it is horizontal and diagonal. The relationship need not be based on expertise; it can be based on influence, trade-offs, wealth, etc. In addition, the status of the relationship need not be differential; it can be equal. Because of these traits, networking has a great potential for being successful. Under networking, then, students could make contact with regents, and faculty on one campus can link up with faculty on other campuses. Networking activity is best used for information sharing and carrying out joint but short-term agenda items.

The third connecting strategy is an offshoot of networking. It is developing *ad hoc relationships*. These ad hoc relationships can be as tightly coupled as partnerships or as loosely coupled as collaborations. In between these two extremes are such relationships as formal associations, coalitions, cooperatives, consortia, and so forth. By using these linkages, individuals and/or small groups increase their strength to influence the agenda they are interested in affecting. They gain respect, credability, and potential resources. And with ad hoc arrangements, people of color could join with unlikely groups, becoming allies on one issue of common import, but separating on other issues. For example, people of color can come together with gays and lesbians on affirmative rights and with conservatives on holding legislators accountable.

REFERENCES

Blackwell, J. E. (1983). Strategies for improving the status of Blacks in higher education. *Planning and Change, 14*(1), 56–73.

Blackwell, J. E. (1989). Mentoring: An action strategy for increasing minority faculty. *Academe, 75*(5), 8–14.

Carter, D. J., & Wilson, R. (1992). *Minorities in higher education; 1991 tenth annual status report.* Washington, DC: American Council on Education.

Evangelauf, J. (1988, September 28). Minority groups continue gains on admission tests. *The Chronicle of Higher Education, 35,* A1.

Hurtado, A., Figueroa, R., & Garcia E. (1996). *Strategic interventions in education: Expanding the Latin/Latino pipeline.* Santa Cruz: University of California Press.

Manzo, K. K. (1993). SAT scores continue recent trends. *Black issues in higher education, 11*(11).

Olivas, Michael A. (1986). *Latino college students.* New York: Teachers College Press.

Sergiovanni, T., & Starratt, R. (1991). *Emerging patterns of supervision: Human perspectives.* New York: McGraw Hill.

U.S. Bureau of the Census. (1990a). *Household and family characteristics, January 1990 and 1989.* Washington, DC: Government Printing Office.

U.S. Bureau of the Census. (1990b, January). *Projections of the population of states by age, sex and race: 1989 to 2010.* Washington, DC: Government Printing Office.

Watkins, B. T. (1988, December 14). Participation of minority students rises 32 points in advanced placement tests. *The Chronicle of Higher Education, 35*(12), A1.

PART II

Administrators' Perspectives

Five Recommendations to Build a Multicultural Campus

Administrator—Chancellor Chang-Lin Tien

- Senior administrators of color must *draw* from the wisdom of their traditional culture and the range of experiences in their lives.

- Senior administrators should take *advantage* of higher education's current self-examination to infuse insights from diverse groups.

- Senior administrators of color should *anticipate* opposition but *commit* to working collaboratively to achieve shared missions and goals of the institution.

- Senior administrators of color must *use* their status to influence increased understanding and improved relations among different groups.

- Senior administrators of color must take an *active* role in all fund-raising efforts to illustrate that success in this area is not limited to white males.

Two

Challenges and Opportunities
for Leaders of Color

Academic leaders of color face critical questions. What role will racial, ethnic, and cultural heritages play in our efforts to guide American universities and colleges? Will we rely on our background as racial minorities as an asset? Or is our heritage a handicap, something to be masked in the hope of avoiding possible conflict and controversy?

The response might seem obvious when the prevailing philosophy today emphasizes that we take pride in our roots, whether our heritage is African, European, Latino, Asian, or Native American. Yet the reality differs from the rhetoric. Although Americans have made tremendous progress, we still do not live in a color-blind society where racial, ethnic, and cultural differences are never considered. Leaders who do not fit the traditional mold run into resistance. This is especially true in the academic world. No matter how much we like to consider ourselves a force for change, colleges and universities are still constrained by thousands of years of tradition.

Being of Asian heritage did not always seem to be a clear advantage. Asian Americans are a relatively new force in higher education. American colleges and universities have seldom looked to Asia for inspiration. Higher education in the United States traces its roots to European traditions and institutions, starting with Plato's Academy, then the professional and theological schools in Paris, Bologna, and Salerno that arose during the Middle Ages, and continuing with Oxford, Cambridge, and the great German research universities.

Until recently, Asian Americans didn't enjoy significant influence on the faculties and administration of U.S. universities. In 1969, only 1.3% of the nation's professors were Asian Americans. By the 1990s, that has grown to 5.1%. Asian Americans are starting to head major colleges and universities as well. After my appointment as chancellor of the University of California, Berkeley, in 1990, Henry T. Yang was named chancellor of the University of California at Santa Barbara, and David Chang became president of Polytechnic University in New York. Both appointments took place in 1994.

The role of Asian American leaders is made more complicated by the rising tide of anti-immigrant fervor. At one time, America proudly proclaimed that it was built by immigrants. Now, newcomers are increasingly feeling shame, especially those from Latin America, Asia, and the Middle East. Being native born is no protection against scapegoating. Many Americans assume that people with Asian, Latino, or Middle Eastern features must be recent immigrants.

My distinctive Chinese accent leaves no doubt about my origins. While British, German, and French accents are acceptable or even prestigious in academic circles, Asian and Latino inflections are problematic. A European inflection conjures up images of Oxford, Cambridge, or the belles lettres. In contrast, an Asian or Latino accent is more likely to be considered an indication of a lack of schooling. Yet, from the start of my career, I have relied on my Chinese heritage as a strength. The wisdom of my traditional culture and the range of experiences in my life as an immigrant and naturalized American have enriched my insights and increased my ability to confront the challenges in higher education. Instead of regarding my heritage as a drawback, I view it as an extra resource, something that I wouldn't be able to enjoy if I weren't a racial minority.

My approach to leadership stems from my Chinese background. The Chinese character for crisis is comprised of two characters: one stands for danger and the other for opportunity. For me, times of crisis present both challenges and opportunities. This is a departure from the Western view, which regards crises primarily as difficulties and hardships.

What distinguishes a great leader? In times of crisis, the good leader knows how to meet the challenges. Only the great leader takes advantage of the unique opportunities as well.

This approach to leadership has served me well as powerful forces transform our world and pose unprecedented challenges for U.S. higher education. The information revolution, globalization of the world community, rapid diversification of the nation's population, and the international drive for democracy are forcing colleges and universities to undergo intensive self-examination and restructuring. Instead of being tempted to ignore the challenges in the vain hope they will disappear, I am always looking for the opportunities.

I took the same approach to the challenge of being the first Asian American to head a major U.S. university. Although it would be easy for me to rage against the myths and stereotypes about Asian Americans, I believe this would ultimately be self-defeating. Instead, I concentrate on the opportunities. As the first Asian American chancellor of a major research university in the United States, I have the rare opportunity to set high standards and show the world the kind of contributions that Asian American leaders can make in preparing higher education for the twenty-first century.

This essay will focus on approaches and strategies I have used that have been influenced by my heritage. I will discuss: how my reliance on traditional Chinese values helped me make decisions, handle conflicts, and respond to racial discrimination; how I learned to be an effective and persuasive communicator even with a distinct accent; how Chinese values helped me create a more humane institution; how my concentration on building athletics and fund-raising programs contributed to overturning stereotypes of Asian Americans; and how my commitment to diversity in higher education is reflected in student outreach efforts and curricular changes that prepare undergraduates for the diverse world of the next century.

For me, America is the land of opportunity. This is not merely a dream, but my experience. No other nation in the world has welcomed immigrants like me to its shores, offered us first-rate schooling, and then accepted our professional contributions. As I have climbed in college administration, I have relied on the grand American tradition of democracy and the extraordinary emphasis on equality among women and men as my foundation.

My Chinese heritage strengthens this foundation. I consider myself lucky to be an American of Asian heritage.

The Role of Traditional Chinese Values

A simple banner hanging next to my desk reminds me that the basic tenets of traditional Chinese philosophy are an important element in my professional life. Against the banner's white background are flowing Chinese characters in black ink. Although these characters actually stand for the Zen school of Buddhism, to me they symbolize the importance of acting in a way that satisfies my conscience and brings me inner peace and harmony.

Making decisions is a central part of leadership. In fact, the power to make decisions defines a leader. Even failure to act is a decision, because inaction yields consequences as definite as taking action. It is also true that every decision creates support and opposition.

Every decision I make must be right. The right decision isn't necessarily one that will increase my popularity or improve my personal status. Rather, it's the one that I think is the best for Berkeley and higher education at that time. Only by making decisions this way can I satisfy my conscience, maintain inner peace, and live a harmonious life. This is my objective, which always takes precedence over career advancement and material success.

Related to this is my personal emphasis on treating people with respect. Whether I am interacting with a University of California Regent, a state lawmaker, a faculty colleague, a prospective million-dollar donor, or a member of the freshman class, I always show respect. By respect, I mean something more than refraining from name calling and four-letter words, even though this can be tempting at a time when college bashing has become a popular sport. I believe that I must treat each individual with respect even when we disagree on specific issues.

Involved in this respect is showing people that I trust them and have confidence in their ability and commitment to our shared academic mission. Openness is also part of respectful interactions. I voice my differences directly to those I oppose rather than going behind their backs or taking the dispute to the mass media.

Infusing transactions with respect is a central element of my job. At a campus like Berkeley, where conflict and controversy are almost as abundant as Nobel prizes, every position the chancellor takes is sure to stir up a hornet's nest. Whether the topic is diversifying the faculty or raising parking fees, people care. Wherever I weigh in, I can count on opposition, as well as support.

Instead of questioning the motives and morals of my opponents on an issue, I show them I respect them as individuals even when I take issue with their stand. With this approach, I can continue to cooperate closely with those who have opposed me at some time.

Battles come and go, but close colleagues are hard to replace. I treasure the faculty, students, staff, alumni, regents, and fellow administrators who are responsible for making our university great. I cannot afford to let a disagreement get in the way of their support for our shared mission in teaching, research, and public service.

One example of treating opponents with respect occurred in 1992, during a strike of Berkeley graduate student instructors who sought collective bargaining rights. The picket lines of chanting graduate students at major entrances to the campus heightened tensions to a feverish pitch. Thousands of undergraduates refused to cross the picket lines, supporting their student instructors. Scores of professors also supported collective bargaining rights for student instructors.

I opposed the drive for collective bargaining rights. State regulations strictly prohibit recognizing unions that represent students in collective bargaining, and, as chancellor, I am responsible for upholding state law. Even more important, though, is my conviction that collective bargaining rights in this case would have created more problems than solutions. Yet, despite my opposition to union recognition, I understand the tremendous problems graduate students face and I value their enormous contribution to the university. When I was a graduate student, I also faced the challenge of balancing an incredible work load of research, teaching, and studying, while somehow making financial ends meet. Today's graduate students face the additional hardship of a tight job market and shrinking research support.

Throughout the weeks-long protest, my administration continued to show respect to picketing students and their all-too-real concerns about the hardships shared by graduate student instructors. Our statements to the press and internal publications made it clear that even though we disagreed with collective bargaining rights as a solution, we recognized the problems leading up to the strike. We also expressed our willingness to work collaboratively with graduate students on addressing the problems. At the height of the protest, I even went to the picket lines and talked directly with students to make sure they understood that I shared their concerns and respected their role at Berkeley—as well as respected their right to protest.

Finally, the protest ran out of steam. Although the strike led to some deep divisions, most of the wounds have healed. In large part, I believe our sense of community has grown stronger because of the mutual respect that has become the hallmark of transactions on campus.

My adherence to traditional Chinese values has also affected the way I have responded to discrimination. I believe it is critical for leaders of color to respond forcefully and positively to racial and ethnic discrimination. Although our status as leaders does not make us immune to discrimination, we do have a stronger voice. We can use our influence to increase understanding and improve relations among the different races and ethnicities in America.

In 1992, my second year as chancellor, I was targeted at a highly visible event. As I approached the podium at a victory rally after a postseason bowl game, a few people from the rival university started to chant: "Buy American." I did not immediately understand what they were doing, so I did not respond during my remarks at the rally.

But I didn't ignore or shy away from this ugly incident. Instead, I used it to increase understanding of how all Americans—not just Americans of Asian descent—suffer when bigotry is allowed to persist. The *Los Angeles Times* and other major newspapers ran stories on a speech that I delivered in Sacramento on February 24, 1992, showing how global economic competition and change have heightened fear among Americans. In this speech, I urged that support for colleges and universities be increased to further understanding and address the underlying problems that concern Americans. Later, I discussed the "Buy American" incident in articles and opinion pieces to emphasize my point that the trend of scapegoating immigrants hurts America, which traditionally has prided itself on being a nation of immigrants. (See, for instance, "America's scapegoats: Immigrant-bashing is hurting the native and foreign born alike," in the October 31, 1994, edition of *Newsweek*.)

I have never allowed myself to respond to racial bigotry with anger or fear. Instead, I address the problem with respect and follow through in a way that satisfies my conscience. As an academic leader of color, I have found that the challenge of racial discrimination can be turned into an opportunity for positive change.

Effective Communications—With a Chinese Accent

Since I arrived in the United States in 1956 to begin graduate studies, communication has been a central issue in my life. Although I started studying English grammar and vocabulary in the third grade, my classes in China did not emphasize conversational skills. So, during my years at American colleges, I had to concentrate on becoming proficient in communicating with professors, fellow students, and undergraduates.

The importance of communications intensified when I joined the Berkeley faculty in 1959, just three years after I arrived in America. My foremost concern was teaching. It was essential that students grasp fully the content of my lectures. Equally important was encouraging free exchange in class. I wanted my students to feel free to ask questions and air their ideas.

Like all new faculty, I devoted hundreds of hours to preparing for classes. With the additional challenge of my Chinese accent, I carefully outlined each lecture in detail. Then I practiced delivery. Often I rehearsed until midnight or later, with my patient wife serving as audience and critic. By the time of the actual class, I felt fully organized and prepared.

The response from my students was gratifying. They said my classes increased their understanding of highly complex topics in mechanical engineering. The tight organization of the lectures helped them digest even the most difficult subjects. My success in communications was reinforced when I received a Distinguished Teaching Award in 1962, the youngest professor to receive this campus honor—a campus record that is still unbroken.

The issue of my Chinese accent surfaced again following my appointment as Berkeley chancellor in 1990. A few friends and alumni who supported me offered to pay for coaching to eliminate my Asian accent. These well-intentioned offers put me in a delicate position. It was clear that I must be a powerful and persuasive communicator as Berkeley chancellor. Yet I knew that efforts to eradicate my accent would send a strong signal to the Asian American community that I was embarrassed by my heritage, a reaction similar to the response of African Americans to Black rock stars who bleach their skin. Moreover, such an effort could easily be interpreted by immigrants as shame of being foreign born.

I took the same course that I followed as a young professor. I would make communication a priority by striving to be clear, precise, and highly organized. Instead of trying to eliminate my accent, I would turn it into an asset. My accent makes me stand out in the academic world. So, it is easy to single me out and remember me. In this era of information overload, this is a great advantage when I try to drive home some critical messages about Berkeley and higher education.

Also, I have found that my accent and my heritage can help put people at ease who otherwise might feel uncomfortable in academic settings. For instance, counselors who run Berkeley's outreach programs aimed at African American and Latino secondary-school students take interest in how I interact easily with youths and their parents.

Before and after making presentations at conferences and seminars, I enjoy talking informally one-on-one or in small groups with teens and their families who often have no prior experience with colleges. Although I like to meet people and hear their views as a matter of course, our outreach counselors advise me that many high-ranking officials don't mingle with these audiences as easily. My personal style and accent make people who are attending their first college event feel more comfortable. As a result, I believe that Berkeley seems less remote and forbidding, which is important in our drive to recruit the most academically talented students who reflect the rich diversity of California.

The way I speak reinforces my background as an immigrant. This helps me to speak forcefully on issues affecting immigrants. The recent trend to blame immigrants for many of America's problems is highly disturbing. Hundreds of state and federal measures have been introduced to curb legal and illegal immigration. Backers of these proposals often rely on inflammatory anti-immigrant rhetoric to grab attention and move Americans to action. Although I agree that controlling the volume of immigration is important, I think some Americans are forgetting that our nation was built by immigrants and that our immigrant heritage is the wellspring of our nation's strength and vitality.

As a naturalized American who has encountered anti-immigrant hostility, I am in a good position to take a stand in the national debate on immigration. I am proud that my writings and interviews with print and broadcast media have influenced the tone of the dialogue on immigration and have served as a reminder of America's immigrant roots.

More Human Interactions, Less Red Tape

Virtually every new leader vows to cut bureaucracy and infuse their institution with a more humane element. In all too many cases, though, this pledge is forgotten in the crush of daily demands, crises, and conflicting outside forces.

One outgrowth of my heritage is my emphasis on dealing with people on a human level. After serving years as chancellor of Berkeley, I can now point out that I do more than give lip service to this objective. I have cut through some of the red tape in order to interact directly with individuals. Moreover, my strong emphasis on restoring the human touch has spread throughout our campus.

No one opposes cutting bureaucracy and making institutions more people oriented. In fact, these interrelated objectives are about as universally accepted as mom and apple pie. So why are these objectives so easy to talk about yet so difficult to accomplish? First, it takes time for officials to interact with people individually and in small groups. Second, it is not particularly glamorous to reduce bureaucratic red tape and put people first. Finally, it is not something you can accomplish overnight; you have to work on it day after day, and so many other seemingly more urgent matters can easily get in the way.

I have given serious consideration to these challenges before crafting my strategy. Like every leader of a major institution, I realize that every second of my time counts. I carefully select those situations that best symbolize how I care about the people who are served by our university as well as the people who make Berkeley run. If I show that the institution's top official cares, people are more likely to feel the institution is putting them first. However, if I can't invest time in a given situation, then I am in danger of sending the message that this is not important enough to warrant the chancellor's attention.

Another approach I have taken is to focus on cutting bureaucracy. Long after most people have forgotten my inaugural address, I continue to talk about the importance of making Berkeley more humane. At first, some faculty and staff probably thought I was simple minded when I repeated the same objectives time and again. Now they know I am serious about meeting these objectives.

Here are some examples that show my strategies for emphasizing the importance of putting people first. One of my first acts as chancellor was to urge that all the departments involved in helping students coordinate services and activities at the start of the school year. When I took office, waiting in long lines at the start of school was considered as inevitable as fog hanging over the San Francisco Bay. Students had to find their way through a maze of procedures to register, enroll in classes, and receive financial aid. This experience reinforced the image of Berkeley as an impenetrable bureaucracy.

Berkeley staff responded to my request right away, putting into action some immediate remedies and planning for long-range, bureaucracy-cutting efforts. To show the depth of my commitment, I devoted several lunch hours at the start of the school year to the information tables set up on Sproul Plaza, the recognized center of student activities. I met hundreds of new students and guided them to appropriate offices. Several members of my administration joined me in this effort. In subsequent years, I continued to make frequent appearances on the front line of student services.

My time has been well spent. There is considerable truth to the old saying that actions speak louder than words. A single lunch time appearance at a back-to-school information table says more about my commitment than a hundred memos on the importance of serving students. Of course, I have had to follow another adage as well. I have put my money where my mouth is, providing funds and administrative support for streamlining and putting admissions, enrollment, registration, and financial aid services on-line.

Times of crisis also provide opportunities for putting a human face on the institution. This was a lesson I learned within months of taking office. In my first year as chancellor, our campus suffered the kind of tragedies at the start of school that could have easily destroyed the finest community-building efforts. In September 1990, 3 students died in a fraternity house fire. Just two weeks later, a mentally unstable gunman killed 1 student and held 18 others hostage for several hours in a popular tavern close to campus.

Parents grieved the loss of children whose bright futures were obliterated overnight in senseless tragedies. Students mourned the loss of friends and classmates. Everyone on campus wondered what the future held. A shadow fell over Berkeley as fear and uncertainty spread across campus.

This was not a time to delegate my responsibility to others. Even the most sensitive words of condolence would fall short of the mark if they were conveyed on paper, not in person. As the top person on campus, I was responsible for sharing in our community's suffering in order for the community to begin the long process of recovery and healing. I accompanied parents to the morgue to identify the bodies of their children. I visited students who were hospitalized after the hostage crisis and met with their families. I led several memorial services. I talked with the staff who were responding to the crisis and personally thanked them for providing an array of support services.

I relied on news conferences and press interviews to communicate with the outside. I issued special statements in campus publications to communicate with the campus. Yet this was not enough. Nothing less than the personal involvement of the chancellor could provide tangible evidence that the university does care. I believe that my personal intervention signified far more to those who suffered during these tragedies than beautifully worded formal statements. My presence also helped reassure the entire campus community. It would have been all too easy for tragedy to tear Berkeley apart. Instead, our sense of community grew even stronger.

When crisis returned two years later, I had no choice about whether to become involved. On the first day of the fall 1992 semester, a young woman broke into my home in the early morning. When she attacked a campus police officer with a machete, police shot and killed her.

Again, tragedy threatened to cloud the start of school. I understood how easily this event could shatter our collective sense of safety and well-being on campus. Some colleagues advised me to cancel all activities and stay out of sight. Instead, in the hours following the break-in, I visited the largest freshman lecture classes. I talked directly with students to reassure them the situation was under control.

We quickly put together a special issue of our campus publication that appeared the next day so that the entire campus community could read a detailed description of events. Also, I was able to convey my message to a larger campus audience. In the August 26, 1992, edition of *The Berkeleyan*, I wrote: "Let us channel the outpouring of support and concern over this tragedy to where it will make a difference. Now is the time for us to work together to create the kind of campus and community where each one of us can work, study, and live confident of our personal safety."

Clearly, personal involvement of leaders during crises is essential. It can be important during daily transactions as well. I often pick up the phone and dial faculty colleagues directly. This may not sound like much, yet this simple act stands out in a world where most executives save time by having their assistants place calls for them. Several professors tell me they are surprised when they hear my voice on the phone right away. Apparently, the symbolism of making my own phone calls is powerful, as the news that I do so has spread around campus. This has convinced more people about my commitment to cutting bureaucracy than countless speeches could do.

My participation also makes a difference in our campaign to recruit the finest professors and retain talented faculty who are wooed by first-class institutions. I try to talk directly with as many top faculty candidates as I can fit into my schedule. It is just as important for me to talk with Berkeley professors who are considering posts elsewhere. Again, I find that personal interaction is highly effective. Both faculty candidates and veterans more readily believe that Berkeley is really interested in them when they hear directly from me.

This approach has inspired similar efforts. For instance, faculty and administrators work in teams to phone exceptional students who have been accepted at Berkeley. We believe these personal calls help convince some applicants to choose Berkeley over other universities. There is another benefit as well. These phone calls show that Berkeley, despite its large size, cares about individual students.

My personal involvement is not only good for the institution; it also keeps me in touch with the currents of campus life. By talking directly to faculty, students, staff, alumni, and parents, I see and hear their concerns firsthand. This interaction gives me a far deeper understanding of the needs and demands that our campus community faces than official reports can offer.

Moving Beyond the Stereotypes

It is hardly surprising that many mistaken notions persist about Asian American academics since we are relative newcomers to higher education. Yet, as the first Asian American to head a major U.S. university, I have not attacked directly the myths about Asian Americans. I believe that responding directly to each stereotype would consume too much time and limit my effectiveness as chancellor. My foremost responsibility is helping Berkeley meet its challenges and take advantage of its opportunities. If my leadership contributes to our campus becoming the model for higher education in the twenty-first century, then some stereotypes about Asian Americans will be overturned along the way.

This has proven to be true during my first years as chancellor. There are two examples of how my efforts to build programs have enjoyed the side benefit of counteracting mistaken notions about Asian Americans. The pervasive stereotype of Asian Americans is that we are inscrutable and mysterious. More recently, as the "model minority" myth has taken hold, we are regarded as "nerds"—serious, hard-working scholars who excel in computers and sciences, but shy away from playing fields.

According to the model-minority stereotype, hard-working Asian Americans concentrate solely on individual achievement; little time is left over for philanthropy and civic responsibilities. If this myth were true, then Asian American leaders would be reluctant to make fundraising campaigns a top priority. Moreover, they would lack the skills for inspiring prospective donors to contribute funds or give their talent and prestige to fund drives.

These stereotypes confronted me as well. Before being appointed chancellor, I learned of two concerns of the regental search committee. First, would I support athletics? Second, could I be successful in fundraising? Support of sports programs and developing sources of funding are serious issues in college administration. A strong athletics program builds spirit on campus, draws favorable national attention, and forges alumni links to their alma mater. Building private and corporate support is critical for university leaders as public support declines steadily.

If it had been up to me to pick two stereotypes of Asian Americans that would be easy to disprove, I couldn't have done any better. Long before I thought of dedicating my life to higher education, I dreamed of becoming a professional basketball star. When I came to the United States, I had to face the fact that at 5 feet, 6 inches, I was not professional material. Even though I turned my full attention to engineering studies, my passion for basketball and other competitive sports didn't fade. As a student and professor, attending sports matches and cheering campus athletes was a wonderful benefit of college life.

As chancellor, my love for sports quickly became known. I attended women's and men's competitions, enjoying every moment of cheering on our teams. My unquestioned support for intercollegiate athletics and intramural club sports has contributed to the growth of our program. Our football team has enjoyed three victories at bowl games. Women and men athletes from Berkeley won six medals in the 1992 Olympics. We are adding three new sports to the intercollegiate women's program, and we are refurbishing our playing facilities.

Today, Berkeley is on the road to a strong sports program that reinforces campus spirit and our sense of community. Who knows? Even a Rose Bowl victory might be around the corner. Moreover, even though I never directly countered the stereotype of nerdy Asian Americans, those who once questioned my interest in sports now realize this Asian American chancellor is a lifelong fan.

Similarly, one of my first objectives when taking office was spearheading the drive for private support. This did not stem from any desire to overturn stereotypes. Instead, I realized that Berkeley had to seek new sources of funding in order to preserve and advance our first-rate teaching, research, and public service.

State support for Berkeley and the entire University of California system has dropped dramatically in the last three decades. In the 1960s, the state provided as much as 75% of our funding. Between 1990 and 1995, state support for the Berkeley campus dropped from 49% to 37%. With these kinds of figures, I didn't need a degree in advanced mathematics to determine that increasing private support would be essential to the future of Berkeley.

Again, this is an area where our campus has enjoyed phenomenal success. In my first five years as chancellor, Berkeley has received more than $100 million annually in private contributions. In the 1994–95 school year, we raised a record $156 million.

This is just the start. We are laying the foundation for a major fundraising drive with an expected goal of $1 billion, the largest in campus history. While typical campaigns focus on securing support for buildings, we hope to concentrate on raising money that will support learning and research. Scholarships, fellowships, and faculty grants are central elements of our planned campaign.

In coming years, I am sure to encounter more stereotypes about Asian Americans. Yet I am confident of overturning these stereotypes if I concentrate on successfully guiding our campus through the challenges and helping Berkeley make the most of the opportunities that lie ahead for American higher education.

Achieving Excellence Through Diversity

"Excellence through diversity" became Berkeley's unofficial motto when I became chancellor. This motto reflects our deep commitment to having a student body, faculty, and staff that reflect all of California. As a land-grant university responsible to our state's taxpayers, our campus has the historic obligation of serving students who encompass the diversity of our state. Yet achieving diversity signifies more than meeting our historic responsibility. Colleges and universities are not offering a first-rate education if we fail to prepare students for the highly diverse world of the twenty-first century.

While it is essential for Americans to have a common understanding of our national history, democratic tradition, and culture, we are not teaching the history of America unless we teach the history of all the peoples who have helped to shape this great nation. I believe schools and colleges must encompass the broad spectrum of experiences, achievements, and outlooks of all Americans in our regular curricula.

Compare our agenda for the information revolution to our plans for a multicultural America. Today no one questions the importance of educating future generations to become computer literate. With the demographic transformation of America, isn't it just as important for future generations to become multiculturally literate?

The best way to build trust and respect is to further understanding. We must teach both the differences and similarities in the history and contributions of diverse groups. Only then will future generations understand how their diverse experiences are woven together in one America.

At Berkeley, a year before I became chancellor, the Academic Senate approved a new graduation requirement aimed at increasing understanding of our multicultural nation. Under our system of shared governance at Berkeley, the faculty members of the Academic Senate approve all courses. In this case, the senate decided that Berkeley undergraduates must complete at least one American Cultures course that compares the experiences of different ethnic groups, including those of white Americans.

Before deciding to impose the requirement, the faculty debated the pros and cons of this proposed course with great intensity. Although a majority of those voting favored American Cultures, many faculty were opposed. This increased the challenges associated with successful implementation of the new requirement.

As chancellor, I made my support clear. I provided funds for the new center that guided implementation of the new American Cultures courses. I discussed the value of the new requirement in talks and writings about diversity.

Although my support is only one factor in the success of the American Cultures courses, I am pleased that my message about the importance of this program has been heard. About 130 professors from 41 departments and programs have been approved to teach American Cultures courses. In preparing to teach these courses, faculty from many disciplines have conducted comparative research that integrates the history, outlook, and achievements of different racial and ethnic groups. Nearly 9,000 students enrolled in

American Cultures classes in 1994–95. Today, it is clear that American Cultures classes are an important part of Berkeley's undergraduate program, and the scholarship inspired by this requirement is enriching learning, not just at Berkeley but also at campuses across the country.

Despite our many successes, the future of excellence through diversity at Berkeley is far from certain. We face the unprecedented challenge of preserving diversity following the regents' decision in July 1995 to end affirmative action at University of California campuses. This action makes the nine campuses the first in the nation to admit students without consideration of race, ethnicity, or gender.

The regents' resolution also calls on the University of California "to develop and support programs which will have the effect of increasing the eligibility rates of groups which are 'underrepresented' in the university's pool of applicants." Despite this support for diversity, many people believed the regents' action sent the message that the University of California no longer cares about serving students who reflect our state. I knew we had to act quickly. One month after the regents' decision, I announced a new program, the "Berkeley Pledge."

At a news conference held at the Media Academy, a nationally recognized training program for high-school journalists based at an urban Oakland, California campus, I appeared with the superintendents of the major urban school districts in our area. We encouraged students of all backgrounds to prepare for college. We assured them that our goal is to make sure money is no obstacle for qualified students who want to enroll at Berkeley. Finally, we pledged to help students succeed in college. In exchange, we urged students in elementary and secondary schools to study, earn good grades, and qualify for Berkeley.

I launched the Berkeley Pledge by committing $1 million of campus funds. I also committed $10,000 of my own income. As part of the pledge, I vowed that Berkeley will: strengthen the partnership with local schools; expand our recruitment of high-school students; work to keep Berkeley affordable; create an environment that will foster success; and inspire students to pursue graduate studies and professional careers. To put the Berkeley Pledge into action, I created task forces and boards that will concentrate on outreach and recruitment.

The initial response has been encouraging. For all of us who believed in the value of affirmative action, the Berkeley Pledge offers a new positive focus. At the same time, we realize that we must monitor our progress closely. Without consideration of race, ethnicity, or gender, it is going to be extremely difficult to maintain the level of diversity. We must evaluate carefully our successes and failures so that we can channel resources into the most effective programs.

"Concentrate on Today"

I have been lucky to enjoy a wonderful foundation that rests on the opportunities and great traditions of America combined with my Chinese heritage. I am also fortunate to have had my father's advice to guide me. Twice broken—by the Japanese invasion of China in the 1930s and the Chinese revolution in the late 1940s—my father had nothing to give me other than his wisdom. As it turns out, his wisdom turned out to be the most valuable of all.

"Concentrate now on doing the best job today," my father told me. "Worry later about what comes next." This is what I try to do. By doing the best possible job I can as Berkeley's chancellor today, I am helping make sure that this campus meets the challenges and mines the opportunities that will arise tomorrow.

Five Recommendations to Build a Multicultural Campus

Administrator
Howard L. Simmons

- Administrators should *develop* and *sponsor special forums and workshops* on diversity and multiculturalism as a part of their mission and primary reason for being.

- Administrators should *include* in the structure of higher education organizations *provisions for subunits* that emphasize multiculturalism as a part of their mission and primary reason for being.

- Administrators should *develop* and *disseminate policy statements and guidelines* related to inclusion and cultural pluralism.

- Administrators should *develop* and *use standards and guidelines* by regional and national accrediting bodies that include requirements and suggestions for creating more multicultural campus environments.

- Administrators should *use media and published materials* to promote diversity and multiculturalism, both directly and indirectly.

Three

External Agents
Fostering Multiculturalism

> Within the context of a commitment to democratic values, the diversity of the world's peoples is to be welcomed, respected, and fostered.   (Hill, 1991, p. 42)

Though colleges and universities exist and function most effectively within a larger environment influencing higher education, one does not always immediately think of the various external agents that are major stakeholders in the development of policies and practices. This is especially true when the issue on campus is fostering multiculturalism and diversity. Thus, in addition to what colleges and universities themselves do to foster multiculturalism in all aspects of academic and student life, the role and impact of a broad range of external agents need to be examined. In this work, these external agents for closer examination include but are not limited to: national and professional associations, especially caucuses and other subunits devoted to multicultural and diversity issues; accrediting bodies and the news media, including academic presses; book publishers; local, state, and federal government agencies; foundations and philanthropic organizations; community organizations; fraternal organizations; business and industry; and, of course, multicultural organizations.

Before examining the role and impact of these external agents and their contributions in fostering multiculturalism and diversity on American college and university campuses, it is important to underscore the value of multiculturalism and diversity to the quality and effectiveness of higher education. Our focus must be on the larger American society in which multiculturalism and diversity, vis-à-vis our population base, is a fact of life; we need not apologize for this. What is more difficult is providing an acceptable definition about what we mean by diversity and multiculturalism. Although most would agree that diversity has always existed in the general population, there is considerable room for disagreement about whether every American college and university campus has achieved or should achieve the goal of diverse student bodies and faculty and multicultural curricula, services, and environments for teaching and learning.

I use the term diversity here to refer to the different racial and ethnic groups, cultures, traditions, and belief systems represented by the constituent groups on and off campus. Multiculturalism, which can be a product of this diversity, is the positive interaction of these groups in which persons within each group are aware of their own cultural heritage and work to understand and appreciate the differences of other cultures and civilizations. And while multiculturalism may not have been achieved on a large number college and university campuses, there is considerable evidence that a number of external agents have played a major role in bringing about more multi-cultural awareness and positive action in American higher education.

I have spent more than 25 years participating in or leading various forms of accrediting activities at regional and national levels. I will use my own expertise and experience as the primary basis for this essay, particularly since diversity and multiculturalism in higher education became a high profile topic primarily due to a controversy started by the U.S. Department of Education over the commitment to diversity by the Middle States Commission on Higher Education. At the time of the fractious debate, much was written about diversity, pluralism, and multiculturalism on American colleges and university campuses, and almost every major conference of national higher education associations devoted a great deal of attention to the topic. But I never published my own assessment of what transpired and how important the actual discussions and outcomes would be for higher education in general, not just for the five hundred plus postsecondary institutions in the Middle States region.

However, now that the commission and its constituents—and the federal government—essentially resolved the local issues and I am some distance from that experience, I believe a review of the academic and leadership issues is important. This effort may be even more relevant in 1997 because of the dismantling of affirmative action programs and the fear of some that attention will no longer be given to diversity principles and commitments to further the cause of multiculturalism on college and university campuses. That is one reason why higher education needs the intervention and support of a variety of external agents to assist in maintaining commitments to diversity and multiculturalism.

The Middle States Case: The Issue of Diversity and Multiculturalism Put to the Test

At the beginning of the 1990s, I had been on the staff of the Middle States Commission on Higher Education for more years than I had ever anticipated. When I accepted the initial offer of employment, I had no idea that, as its executive director, I would be defending the existing standards—committing member colleges and universities to programs of diversity and multiculturalism.

I suppose we just assumed that equity and diversity were facts of life to be dealt with and that multiculturalism would soon follow because persons in higher education accepted the concepts of equity, fairness, and integrity in all institutional endeavors, including but not limited to student admissions, faculty recruitment, academic services, curriculum development, management, and the like. Nevertheless, my 27 years in higher education at the time and my more than 20 years of being involved in the accreditation process suggested to me that, by their very nature, some issues were recurrent and potentially explosive—especially since they would be given greater prominence by political and other external forces. As you will see, they were both challenge and opportunity for me, the Middle States Association, and the rest of higher education.

It is instructive to start by (1) clarifying the position of the Middle States Association regarding diversity and multiculturalism, especially in collegiate learning environments; (2) addressing some of the misconceptions and uninformed observations that had been poorly articulated in the media and elsewhere about diversity and multiculturalism as espoused by regional accrediting bodies; and (3) suggesting why it is defensible and essential for regional accrediting bodies to foster equity, diversity, and multiculturalism in their own activities and in collegiate learning environments.

Because these purposes are interrelated, I have not addressed them in a serial fashion. In addition, as indicated earlier, diversity and multiculturalism have innumerable and conflicting meanings and applications, but an added emphasis here is on equity. As defined by Webster, "equity" represents principles of fairness, impartiality, and justice. And diversity in this context, while emphasizing differences, focuses on inclusion. As Professor Sylvia Hurtado (1996, p. 27) points out: "A climate of inclusion has a positive effect on learning outcomes." She states further that "many campuses were not prepared for the changes they would undergo as a result of including more adult students, women, and racial/ethnic minorities in their student bodies. These changes in student enrollments were connected with major intellectual and social movements that raised important questions about the production and transmission of knowledge, as well as access to education" (p. 27).

From the perspective of this case of an accrediting body committed to fostering diversity and multiculturalism, such questions definitely are related to the quality and integrity of programs and services offered by accredited institutions. Again, reflecting on the lively and often difficult discussion of the real and perceived issues in the Middle States case, it is even clearer now that a significant group in higher education perceived "diversity" and "multiculturalism" as code words for quotas or political correctness. In a report that studied how students might be affected by diversity and multi-culturalism on campus, Alexander Astin (1993, p. 44) described the situation in this fashion: "Amidst debates over multiculturalism, diversity, and political correctness by academics and the news media, claims and counter-claims about the dangers and benefits of multiculturalism have abounded, but so far little hard evidence has been produced to support any of these claims."

That is precisely why many in higher education concluded that what had happened at Middle States was primarily responsible for an accentuation of the debate over diversity, multiculturalism, and political correctness. The latter seemed to be a cause célèbre for self-anointed and ultraconservative groups like the National Association of Scholars. This group was allegedly quite persuasive with the Bush administration and then Secretary of Education Lamar Alexander in initiating action against the Middle States Association for expecting its member institutions to foster diversity and multiculturalism. The sad truth was that the rather general, innocuous references in the agency's standards—long approved by the Middle States constituency—had been designed to ensure equitable treatment for all students, including traditionally underrepresented persons such as African Americans, Hispanics (for example, Chicanos, Puerto Ricans, Dominicans), Native Americans, Asian Americans, and women.

Whether out of fear or some other motivation, some raised the specter of quotas as inflammatory rhetoric. Based on the facts of Middle States' situation, there was absolutely no basis for concluding that token representation of minorities or women was a threat to existing power bases in the academy. That is, the Middle States Commission on Higher Education had not removed or seriously threatened to remove the accreditation of a member institution because it had not complied with some quota system that never existed.

Therefore, the Middle States and its constituent institutions not only engaged in new debates about principles and standards earlier agreed to, they also resolved to defend the rights and freedoms of all students and faculty. In essence, they concluded once again that the terms "diversity" and "multiculturalism" implied inclusion rather than exclusion. Similarly, as the executive director of the commission, I was convinced that no respected leader in higher education would seriously suggest that we did not live in an increasingly diverse American society, a global society, and interdependent world. Further, I was convinced that those of us in the accrediting universe and elsewhere were aware of the rapidly changing demographics in higher education and that most of us had an abiding concern about student access and success based on strong considerations for equity and quality.

At the time, it was also important for higher education leaders not to be coy about what was meant by fostering diversity and multiculturalism in the academy. They needed to continue to assert that diversity already existed because there was a spectrum of institutions (two- and four-year colleges, private and public institutions, church-related colleges, historically Black colleges and universities, or traditionally single-sex colleges, among others). Those forms of institutional diversity had always been the reality, and accrediting bodies not only welcomed them but believed that this diversity enriched and added to the quality of American higher education. However, most of us appreciated that if we were really addressing this type of diversity, it would have been unlikely that we would have been focusing so intensely on the value and appropriateness of diversity and multiculturalism in determining institutional quality and effectiveness. Even the admission of the opposite sex to traditional single-sex institutions had not met with such strong reactions at that time. However, when the emphasis shifted to equity and diversity for underrepresented persons and protected groups, the "difficult dialogues" began. What was encouraging was that both productive dialogues and positive action related to the topic of diversity were well underway.

But was the mere presence of underrepresented persons of color and women on campus the real reason for much of the seemingly interminable debate over diversity and multiculturalism? Again, the facts in the Middle States case would suggest no. Important in the scheme of things was what happened when increased diversity was already a reality; this meant that the principle of equity applied to all of the culturally different newcomers. It was hoped they had been recruited, enrolled, or employed with the same commitment to their particular needs and with the same commitment to their retention and success as students, faculty, or staff.

That brings us to the other extremely important criterion for equity, diversity, and multiculturalism—the consideration of campus climate or environment as it impacts on the teaching and learning process. We were already painfully aware that it did no good at all to attract, recruit, and enroll any students—especially those who were culturally different—to campus environments that were inhospitable or that had college officials who were not willing to make some adjustments to accommodate the different but rich qualities of the new arrivals. Perhaps it would have been better in some cases if colleges or universities had not been so vigorous in recruiting such students until they had prepared their environments appropriately for the changes.

But that was left to the accredited institution to decide. Accrediting bodies were more concerned—as they indeed should have been—with the integrity and equitable application of an institution's recruitment and admissions policies, to assure that all students were treated fairly.

The other aspect of the campus climate that the Middle States Association—and most likely other regional accrediting bodies—would have been concerned about was the increase in campus violence and tension, which affects the teaching and learning processes as well as student progress and achievement. And since some of the tension was likely the result of increased diversity and growing insensitivity of one group to another, accrediting bodies had to assess how effective the institution was in developing and implementing policies that helped alleviate such potential threats to student academic progress. It would have been tragic indeed if student outcomes suggested that graduates were technically qualified but unprepared to live and work in a culturally diverse world. Most formal mission statements themselves were explicit about expectations that graduates should have the qualities necessary to live in a pluralistic and interdependent world.

This was occurring at a time when accrediting bodies, concerned about finding a more satisfactory means of improving quality and assessing the effectiveness of colleges and universities, had embraced outcomes strategies as a means for institutions to improve their overall performance. Regrettably, some critics suggested that a simultaneous focus on quality improvement and principles of diversity and multiculturalism were somehow mutually exclusive. The results of a significant study on equity and diversity as reflected in *Achieving quality and diversity: Universities in a multicultural society* (Richardson & Skinner, 1991) suggest a different scenario by concluding "that institutions can achieve both quality and diversity through adaptations that support achievement by more diverse learners."

What are some of the factors that enable an accrediting body to foster diversity and multiculturalism in learning environments? The first should be fairly obvious. Before any accrediting body can promote principles of equity and diversity on the campuses it accredits, it must already be committed to the same principles and its policies and practices should reflect that. In other words, they should practice what they preach. However, the report of a national study (Simmons, Bender, & Myers, 1986) on *Involvement and empowerment of minorities and women in the accrediting process* concluded that, with few exceptions, regional accrediting bodies also needed to reflect greater diversity on their staffs and in their accrediting protocols. Just as representation and inclusiveness are important factors in the make-up of student bodies, faculties, staffs, and governing boards, they are also important in assuring that commissions, committees, and evaluation teams reflect the constituency being served.

The second factor, and perhaps the most crucial to the accrediting body's effective fostering of diversity and multiculturalism, is in the statements of mission and goals of most institutions. It is rare, indeed, when an institutional mission statement doesn't contain explicit or implicit language about justice, equity, pluralism, and the need for students and graduates to be fully cognizant of the global and interdependent society in which we live. But rather than indicting institutions for the situation as it is, it should be clear that, up to now, accrediting bodies haven't generally held their member institutions accountable for these aspects of the mission statements.

The importance of addressing the issue of mission and goals when one is considering the concepts of diversity and multiculturalism in the accrediting process cannot be overstated. It is a fairly well-understood and accepted principle in the accrediting world that the primary basis for evaluating and assessing the effectiveness of an institution is its statement of mission, goals, and objectives. Further, the embodiment of these principles in the mission statements would suggest that they have the potential of impacting all aspects of an institution's operations and raisons d'être. Therefore, it was as inappropriate then as it is now to refer to principles of inclusion and multiculturalism simply as "diversity standards."

Principles of equity, diversity, multiculturalism, and inclusion as applied to collegiate learning environments should be viewed more as principles of integrity and ethical behavior. And that is precisely why the constituency of the Middle States Association—after careful and thoughtful deliberation— decided that these principles were of such importance that they should permeate the entire body of accrediting standards (see Commission on Higher Education, 1994). Just as accrediting bodies promote institutional improvements based on mission and goals in a wide array of programs, services, and activities, some conclude also that they have a corresponding responsibility to ensure that values such as democratic pluralism promulgated by these institutions are likewise assessed.

The onus is on the institution—not the accrediting body—to document its successes in achieving its mission, goals, and objectives, but the regional accrediting body has a corresponding responsibility. That responsibility is to ensure that each accredited and candidate institution is accountable for its mission and goals. Further, the policies and practices of each accredited and candidate institution are to be commensurate with those statements that rest on essential principles of justice, equity, and the respect for the human dignity of all who are legitimately a part of the campus community.

With such a scenario, what accrediting body or accredited institution would dare not develop and implement programs, services, policies, and practices consistent with the total mission? Would dare not assess total institutional effectiveness based on principles of equity, integrity, and other principles as contained in formal statements of mission, goals, and objectives? Would dare not document how it would serve the particular needs and cultural differences of all those recruited, enrolled, employed, or appointed? Would dare not insist on the creation and maintenance of a teaching and learning environment that is virtually free of unconscionable insensitivities to individuals and groups that include abhorrent acts of racism, sexism, bigotry, and violence? Would dare not develop and implement programs and curricula that have academic integrity and whose content provides an accurate reflection of the cultural diversity that characterizes our American culture, Western civilization, and global society? Would dare not insist that the assessment of student learning outcomes take into account the rich cultural heritage represented by both majority and minority students? Would dare not insist that recruitment and hiring policies are based on principles of equity, fairness, and impartiality, and that only the quality essential to the pursuit of particular learning, teaching, or management objectives are considered in the assessment of an individual's suitability for enrollment or employment? Would dare not insist on a program of outcomes assessment that takes into account the particular learning styles and other positive characteristics of all students, including those who happen to be culturally different in a particular setting? Finally, what accrediting body or accredited institution would not continually insist on the maintenance and improvement of quality for increasingly diverse student bodies, faculties, and staffs?

Creating more culturally diverse campuses and achieving more qualitative outcomes are not mutually exclusive, although this charge has often been leveled at institutions and agencies that espouse diversity, inclusion, and multiculturalism. For numerous reasons, most institutions of higher learning in the United States have come to realize that equity and diversity are not code words for quotas or preference, but are American democratic principles that now should extend more clearly to people of color and other groups, just as they were extended to "majority ethnics" who were once labeled cultural "minorities." Now, with the backdrop of the academic and moral considerations in the Middle States case, what were some of the strategies used (or are still available to be used) by the Middle States Association and other peer-accrediting groups to promote diversity and multiculturalism?

These strategies focused on leadership, public communication, opportunities for agency/constituency interaction, and policy development.

The Middle States Case: Strategies for Fostering Diversity and Multiculturalism

- There was a deliberate decision by the Middle States Association and its Commission on Higher Education during the diversity debate to designate association officers and the commission's Executive Committee to serve as spokespersons for the organization. It was apparent to me that this was a necessary strategy so that the focus of the debate would shift from the issues to the chief executive officer, who happened to be a person of color.

- The leadership role played by the executive director of the agency was to be academic, especially in interpreting the agency's standards to internal and external constituent groups as well as to other members of the higher education community (for example, serving as keynote speaker for state, regional, and national conferences) and in workshops concerned with the topics of diversity and multiculturalism.

- In terms of public communication—especially to protect the good name and reputation of the Middle States Association and Commission—the chair of the commission recommended and the Executive Committee agreed to hire a public relations consultant to advise on handling relations with the media and the federal government. This strategy proved to be not only wise but indispensable in gaining access to the editorial boards of major newspapers and magazines, which would be difficult to achieve without such expert assistance. In addition, assistance was provided in writing letters to the editor and op-ed pieces, and in assuring that this information would be disseminated to the widest audience possible.

- Because the development and approval of standards—including the commission's attention to diversity and multiculturalism as factors in the determination of institutional effectiveness—was the prerogative of constituent institutional members, another effective strategy was convening membership forums and focus groups for the purpose of reviewing, making changes, and reaffirming standards.

- The commission authorized the appointment of a national advisory committee to develop a position statement on the application of principles of equity, diversity, and multiculturalism in the evaluation and accreditation process. This strategy resulted not only in a position statement that was ultimately adopted by the Middle States membership, but it also spawned the development of related guidelines to be used in institutional self-study processes.

As a part of its systematic policy-approval process, the commission made diversity and multiculturalism top priorities in the review and readoption of the standards used to evaluate member institutions. It is important to note that actions of the constituencies served not only to reaffirm the standards relating to these issues but also to strengthen them.

The Role and Impact of Other Accrediting Bodies

Also active in fostering diversity and multiculturalism were the Western Association of Schools and Colleges (Accrediting Commission for Community and Junior Colleges and Accrediting Commission for Senior Colleges and Universities) and the Commission on Institutions of Higher Education of the North Central Association of Colleges and Schools. Each accrediting agency organized and conducted discussions with large constituent groups about diversity and multicultural issues and how these issues were important to the determination of quality and institutional effectiveness.

After considerable discussion with its constituent members, the North Central Association's Commission on Institutions of Higher Education adopted a policy statement on diversity. Moreover, the Accrediting Commission for Senior Colleges and Universities, through the leadership of its executive director and chair, collaborated with the American Council on Education and ORYX Press in producing a detailed campus guide on diversity. This publication, which was the result of The Project on Campus Community and Diversity made possible through a grant from The James Irvine Foundation, is entitled *Dialogues for diversity*. In the Preface, the authors (Gerth & Weiner, 1994) make it clear that

[t]his is not yet another book arguing the case or acknowledging the importance of ethnic diversity for the future of American higher education. That case has been made, and eloquently, by many others. These materials are, rather, intended to help groups of individuals on campus toward focused discussion of the role of ethnic diversity in the daily life of colleges and universities. The aim is to help such groups to find their own common ground, not to tell them what that common ground should be. . . . The role of the Commission in connection with these *Dialogues* has been to sponsor the efforts that have gone into their preparation as a service to member institutions, not as a mandate.

It was within this context that another higher education accrediting commission had gone a step further to assist colleges and universities in fostering multiculturalism and diversity—but no less important in fostering diversity and multiculturalism.

The Role and Influence of National Higher
Education Associations

Quite independently of higher education accrediting commissions, a significant number of the national higher education associations joined what had become a protracted national debate over the role and appropriateness of diversity and multiculturalism. Responding to calls from their membership and eager to take the pulse of their members regarding issues that had become extremely sensitive in the academy, these associations not only filled the programs of their annual conferences and meetings with a wide range of topics dealing with diversity and multiculturalism, but some also adopted resolutions or issued policy statements on diversity and multiculturalism. Led by the then activist American Council on Education President Robert Atwell—who earlier had provided a strong and positive response supporting the position of the Middle States Association on diversity—other associations at One Dupont Circle and elsewhere around the Washington beltway caucused about the best way to respond to issues of diversity, inclusion, and political correctness.

The precipitating incident involving the Middle States Association occurred almost seven years ago, but national higher education associations have continued to refine their own public policy statements on diversity and multiculturalism. For example, the American Council on Education, in collaboration with the Association of American Colleges and Universities and the Ford Foundation's Campus Diversity Initiative, still sponsors an annual conference on diversity and multiculturalism. This year's conference, "Educating one-third of a nation VI: Diversity, opportunity, and American achievement" and those that preceded it, had as one of its goals: "to promote institutional change by focusing on diversity in the curriculum, student life, teaching and employment" (American Council on Education, 1997)

A similar goal is reflected in the "Statement of Inclusion" adopted in spring 1997 by the American Association of Community Colleges. Among other things, the statement indicates that "[community] colleges value diversity as an enhancement of . . . experiences in their classrooms, administrative offices, and board rooms" (AACC, 1997).

However, minority and women caucuses, recognized by most of the national associations, have been the most active in fostering diversity and multiculturalism in colleges and universities. This is especially true of the Black, Hispanic, Asian, and Women's caucuses of the American Association for Higher Education (AAHE)—one of the few national associations with individual rather than exclusively institutional memberships. These caucuses, which represent a broad range of personnel from college and university campuses, continue to be instrumental in ensuring that diversity and multiculturalism are seriously considered as key forum topics. Although it is still difficult to conclude that most campuses have embraced diversity or succeeded in achieving multiculturalism in curricula and campus environments, national associations and their subunits (for example, caucuses) continue to have success in fostering diversity and multiculturalism.

Also from a research perspective, the Education Commission of the States commissioned and promulgated the results of several studies on a broad spectrum of issues related to diversity and multiculturalism. For example, in *Achieving campus diversity: Policies for change* prepared by the ECS National Task Force for Minority Achievement in Higher Education, there is at least one conclusion that the "curriculum [should reflect] the contributions of minority cultures to American life." This statement is significant because it underscores the need for greater academic integrity and relevance in the curriculum.

The Role and Impact of the News Media, Including the Academic Press

Because of the controversial nature of diversity and multiculturalism in the academy and in the general society, there has been and continues to be a heightened interest in these topics both in national and academic presses. Though most issues in higher education do not receive much attention, issues surrounding diversity, cultural pluralism, and multiculturalism are the exception. That is not to say that the articles, editorials, and special features have all been positive or designed to foster multicultural environments on college and university campuses. What it does mean is that newspaper and magazine editors as well as television producers seem to classify a number of diversity and multicultural issues as being newsworthy. For example, national newspapers such as the *New York Times, Washington Post, Wall Street Journal,* and the *Christian Science Monitor* and magazines such as *Time, Newsweek,* and *U.S. News and World Report* have devoted significant space to stories about diversity and multiculturalism.

Although some higher education researchers (Willie, 1992, pp. 70–75) provide useful analyses of how magazines engaged in multiculturalism bashing, in a strange sort of way the bashing not only helped keep discussions of the issue at the forefront but likely also prompted some college and university campuses to reexamine their own positions regarding diversity and multiculturalism. Moreover, not all of the popular press engaged in such bashing. For example, I remember clearly during the intense debate over diversity that several large newspapers, such as *USA Today,* carried editorials and op-ed pieces that were totally supportive of diversity and multiculturalism in higher education. These are indirect ways of fostering multiculturalism in higher education, but they are important in that they help the larger society understand and appreciate the value of inclusion in our increasingly global and interdependent society.

Even more than the popular press, however, the academic press through its magazines, newspapers, books, and newsletters have contributed significantly to fostering multiculturalism in higher education. Chief among these are *The Chronicle of Higher Education, Black Issues in Higher Education, Hispanic Outlook, Change, Educational Record, Journal of Higher Education, Journal of Negro Education,* and *Phi Delta Kappan.* In some, the advocacy for multiculturalism is strong. Take, for instance, the stories that appeared in the January/February 1992 issue of *Change* and in the November 1992 issue of *Phi Delta Kappan.* In these issues, both magazines included special sections on the issues of diversity and multiculturalism (*Change,* 1992; Price, 1992).

While we would expect serial publications like *Black Issues in Higher Education* and *Hispanic Outlook* to place a high priority on reporting and supporting issues of diversity and pluralism, it is precisely because of the mission and focus of these publications that they play a pivotal role in ensuring that multiculturalism stays on the front burner for colleges and universities. *Black Issues in Higher Education* determined that there should be broad dissemination of information about multicultural programs that work. The publication periodically cosponsors with other media outlets satellite telecommunications programs on a variety of topics involving diversity and multiculturalism. The programs include not only relevant contemporary topics, but also an illustrious panel of higher education and community leaders sharing their expertise and experience on those topics.

The Role and Influence of Other External Agents in Fostering Diversity and Multiculturalism in Higher Education

State, Local, and Federal Governments. Government agencies are, by their nature, political in orientation, and higher education cannot count on them to develop policies and legislation or to take actions in support of multiculturalism in higher education. This is especially so when there are serious efforts afoot to cripple or eradicate affirmative action programs. Government agencies are limited generally by what is politically and pragmatically feasible. That is why federal agencies, particularly but not exclusively the U.S. Education Department, generally have to use the rule-making process after legislation is passed to ensure that the regulations address issues not specifically mentioned in the legislation itself. For example, federal administrators favorably disposed to diversity and multiculturalism use the rule-making process to ensure that the regulations provide language accommodating inclusive policies and cultural pluralism. When there have been dominant, ultraconservative high-level persons representing the White House, diversity and multiculturalism fared less well. This was the case of the National Endowment for the Humanities when Lynne Cheney was director of that agency. Specifically, a report recommending changes in the nature and content of the teaching of history was severely criticized as being too politically correct and as lacking in academic rigor.

State approval bodies, particularly higher education agencies empowered to grant degree-granting authority, regularly set guidelines for degrees and curricula that include attention to equity, diversity, pluralism, and multi-cultural curricula. This has been especially true of requirements for work in the humanities and social sciences, and more recently in what needs to be reported in assessing institutional effectiveness. One example of this is the performance review system adopted by the New Jersey Commission on Higher Education, which requires that institutions document their success in enrolling and graduating minority students.

Foundations and Philanthropic Organizations. As indicated above (Ford Foundation's collaboration with the ACE), major foundations and other philanthropic organizations regularly set programmatic directions and grants programs that address issues of diversity and multiculturalism in colleges, universities, and the schools. A close examination of the *Foundations Directory* gives a quick review of the goals and programs of these organiza-tions with regard to fostering diversity and multiculturalism. However, one might not always find the buzz words "diversity" or "multiculturalism" in these foundations' mission statements. In addition to funded projects—both research and applied—the specific foci of scholarship and fellowship projects are on multicultural issues.

In "A perspective on Carnegie Corporation's program, 1983–1997," the chief executive officer (Hamburg, 1997) of Carnegie Corporation of New York summarizes part of the organization's programmatic thrust related to diversity, cultural pluralism, and multiculturalism this way:

> Pivotal institutions such as the family, schools [including colleges and universities], community-based organizations, and the media have the power to shape attitudes and skills toward decent human relations or toward hatred and violence. They can make constructive use of findings from research on intergroup relations and conflict resolution. Education everywhere can convey an accurate concept of a single highly interdependent, worldwide species—a vast extended family that shares fundamental human similarities and a fragile planet. The give-and-take fostered within groups can be extended far beyond childhood toward relations between adults and into larger units of organization, even including international relations. (p. 28)

Clearly, this philanthropic foundation, through its promotional materials, is at least indirectly fostering multiculturalism in educational settings and in the larger society. Others, such as the Ford Foundation and the Kellogg Foundation, continue to promote and fund projects that have as their goal the attainment of a more multicultural academy. For instance, the Kellogg Foundation very recently made available a significant multiple-year grant to fund the Hispanic Border Leadership Institute at Arizona State University, New Mexico State University at Las Cruces, Southwest Texas State University, and Paradise Valley Community College. One of the by-products of this funding is that it will increase the numbers and quality of Hispanic leaders who can more effectively address multicultural, United States–Mexico border issues.

Business and Industry. The strategies used by business and industry are not always as obvious as other external agents in fostering diversity and multiculturalism in higher education. But both engage in a number of activities that directly and indirectly influence the degree to which campuses diversify and become more multicultural. Significant among these are sponsoring career and job fairs on and off campus that help ensure broader access to positions than would otherwise be the case; offering internships to a more diverse group of students who not only indirectly influence the corporate culture but also ultimately influence their own campus cultures; and, equally important, providing financial support by sponsoring campus events initiated by campus multicultural organizations.

Fraternal and Service Organizations. Even though many fraternal and service organizations are still not open to all and cannot be described as multicultural in orientation and service, some provide categorical scholarships to underrepresented groups to assure greater diversity and pluralism on America's college and university campuses. These organizations include groups such as Kiwanis, Rotary, Lions, Masons, Knights of Columbus, Knights of Pythias, Order of Elks, etc., as well as national fraternities and sororities. The latter, especially those whose primary membership consists of people of color, give a great deal of attention to multiculturalism programming and support for campus diversity efforts.

Other Community Organizations. Other external agents that have played a role in fostering diversity and multiculturalism in higher education include organizations such as the YMCA, World Affairs Councils, International Visitors' Exchanges, NAACP, C.O.R.E., La Raza, Habitat for Humanity, churches, and sports groups, among others. The common denominator among all of these organizations is their emphasis on intercultural understanding among groups and on globalization in their programming.

Commonly Used Strategies of External Agents Fostering Multiculturalism and Diversity

While external agents fostering multiculturalism and diversity represent a broad spectrum of interest and activities, many of the strategies that are utilized to assist higher education—especially colleges and universities—to be more multicultural are remarkably similar. These include, but are not limited to:

- Developing and sponsoring special forums and workshops on diversity and multiculturalism at local, state, regional, and national conferences on higher education.

- Including in the structure of higher education organizations provisions for subunits that emphasize diversity and multiculturalism as a part of their mission and primary reason for being (for example, caucuses of the American Association for Higher Education, the National Council on Black American Affairs of the American Association of Community Colleges, etc.).

- Organizational development and dissemination of policy statements and guidelines related to inclusion and cultural pluralism.

- Developing and using standards and guidelines by regional and national accrediting bodies that include requirements and suggestions for creating more diverse and multicultural campus environments.

- The use of media and published materials to promote diversity and multiculturalism, both directly and indirectly (for example, the academic press, national newspapers and journals, cable and closed circuit television, Internet and the World Wide Web, among others.

REFERENCES

American Association of Community Colleges (AACC). (1997, Spring). *Statement of inclusion* (policy statement reprint). Washington, DC: AACC.

American Council on Education (ACE). (1997). *Educating one-third of a nation VI: Diversity, opportunity, and American achievement* (preliminary program brochure). Washington, DC: ACE.

Astin, A. (1993). Diversity and multiculturalism on the campus: How are students affected? *Change, 25*(2), 44.

Commission on Higher Education, Middle States Association of Colleges and Schools. (1994). *Characteristics of excellence in higher education, standards for accreditation.* Philadelphia: MSA Commission on Higher Education.

Education Commission of the States. (1990, December). *Achieving campus diversity: Policies for change.* (Report of National Task Force for Minority Achievement in Higher Education, p. 14). Denver: Education Commission of the States.

Gerth, D., & Weiner, S. (1994). *Dialogues for diversity.* (Report on Campus Community and Diversity of the Accrediting Commission for Senior Colleges and Universities of the Western Association of Schools and Colleges, p. xi). Phoenix: ORYX Press.

Hamburg, D. A. (1997) *A perspective on Carnegie Corporation's program, 1983–1997.* (Reprint from the 1996 Annual Report of the Carnegie Corporation, p. 28). New York: Carnegie Corporation.

Hill, P. J. (1991). Multi-culturalism: The crucial philosophical and organization issues. *Change, 23*(4), 42.

Hurtado, S. (1996). How diversity affects teaching and learning. *Educational Record, 74*(4), 27.

Price, H. B. (1992). Multiculturalism: Myths and realities. *Phi Delta Kappan, 74*(3), 208–225.

Richardson, R. C., & Skinner, E. (1991). *Achieving quality and diversity: Universities in a multicultural society.* New York: ACE/Macmillan.

Simmons, H. L., Bender, L. W., & Myers, C. L. (1986, November). *Involvement and empowerment of minorities and women in the accrediting process: Report of a national study* (pp. 65–69). Tallahassee: Florida State University College of Education.

Willie, C. V. (1992). Multiculturalism bashing by magazines. *Change, 24*(4), pp. 70–75.

Five Recommendations to Build a Multicultural Campus

Administrator—Provost
Enrique (Henry) Trueba

- The provost office must *demonstrate* the university's commitment to diversity by *sponsoring* academic initiatives promoting diversity.

- The provost office must *provide* incentives to academic units to recruit and retain students, staff, and faculty of color.

- The provost office must *reward* the achievements of faculty of color in the promotion and tenure process.

- The provost office must make deans/directors *accountable* for the quality of life in their units with regard to fostering diversity.

- The provost office must *install* a well-organized pipeline between the university and schools that serve diverse populations.

ENRIQUE (HENRY) T. TRUEBA ■

Four

Race and Ethnicity in Academia

With few, if any, ethically convincing prospects for transformation—or even survival—we have become cyber-nomads whose temporary homes become whatever electronic circuitry (if any) is available to us. In our hyper-fragmented and predatory postmodern culture, democracy is secured through the power to control consciousness and semioticize and discipline bodies by mapping and manipulating sounds, images, and information and forcing identity to take refuge in the forms of subjectivity increasingly experienced as isolated and separate from larger social contexts.

(McLaren, 1995, p. 117)

As Paulo Freire (1993) has eloquently stated, "Nâo há mudança sem shonho como nâo há sonho sem esperança." (There is no change without a dream as there is no dream without hope) (p. 91). What keeps our hope alive in the struggle for equity is the understanding of the nature of oppression and our right to regain control of our lives. The concepts of race and ethnicity continue to be at the center of public discourse and passionate political debate in Europe and the Americas, including Latin American countries with populations of European descent.[1] The loss of ethnic consciousness on the part of white Americans is partially explained by the above remarks of McLaren. It is no secret that while the precise biological meaning of race becomes more elusive, the sociocultural meaning takes on new dimensions and becomes central in our daily lives. This is especially so in pluralistic societies that have become de jure integrated racially and ethnically, but de facto segregated and stratified economically and socially. In higher education, these concepts take on special significance and have serious consequences for future generations. In the first part of this chapter I discuss race and ethnicity, particularly in the context of higher education. I then present specific suggestions to improve diversification in higher education.

Race, Ethnicity, and Xenophobia

Physical anthropologists and biologists have essentially discarded race as an operational concept because humans have an infinite number of combinations and permutations of characteristics beyond eyes and skin color, bone structure, weight and stature, distribution of fat, and overall appearance. Medical technology and genetics studies go beyond the chemical and physiological structure of internal organs, blood types, and genes to more fundamental possible combinations of similar and dissimilar traits. People are the products of physical and human environments and of their personal experiences, which tend to leave lasting marks after several generations. And because genetic exchanges and miscegenation have taken place across human groups all over the world, the human species has produced the most diversified and bizarre combinations of both visible and invisible characteristics crossing ethnic and religious groups, nations, and continents. Because of this interplay between ecological, biological, sociocultural, and genetic factors, it is impossible to conceptualize an accurate racial taxonomic system of human groups. In contrast, socially defined concepts of race become vital in human relations and determine norms of interaction, judgments about intelligence, expectations about performance, and daily interaction, thoughts, and behavior.

The social concept of race is also elusive in the abstract, but is fleshed out in specific interactional (and often conflictive) contexts: black versus white, brown versus white, black versus yellow, and others. This elusiveness is compounded because our sociological concept of race often brings ethnicity into the picture, even to the point of using both terms inter-changeably. The word *ethnicity* comes from "ethnos" ("people" in Greek) and it has been the center of anthropological studies for more than a century. Scholars have spent millions of hours collecting information about the languages, cultures, environments, occupations, marriage patterns, family lives, kinship systems, property, laws, and so on of ethnic groups around the world (ethnographies).

The knowledge accumulated by these scholars under the leadership of George Peter Murdock is called the Human Relation Area Files, which is frequently used for cross-cultural studies (ethnology). As an integral part of ethnographic research, scholars used ethnolinguistics or sociolinguistics to make inferences about the way members of ethnic groups think from the way they talk. As immigrants from all over the world become part of modern industrial societies, they bring with them their languages, cultures, and life-styles. Thus, ethnicity, within the contexts of modern industrial societies, is compounded by contacts between the cultures of immigrants and that of mainstream peoples in the larger society.

Ethnic groups in the Western world, especially in Europe and the United States, are socially and culturally stratified subgroups of Americans who are recognized as collectively retaining unique and different characteristics compared to mainstream people (see Trueba, Cheng, & Ima, 1993; Trueba, Jacobs, & Kirton, 1990; Trueba, Rodríguez, Zou, & Cintrón, 1993; Trueba & Zou, 1994). Members of the group view their language, culture, religion, art, values, life-style, family organization, children's socialization, and world view as uniquely linked to their home country and ancestors. At times, physical appearance separates them from the rest of society and from other subgroups in the larger society. Consequently, ethnicity refers to that com-plex set of characteristics of groups who share a historical or mythical common ancestor and maintain their own identity "in contrast or opposition" to mainstream society.

Ethnicity is the other side of the assimilation coin. Common opinion has it that to become a "real" (assimilated) American, one must forget his or her ethnic identity. In Europe, according to the media, birthplace and having several generations of ancestors born in Europe does not guarantee to persons of color (especially those from non-Christian religions) the right to be considered a European citizen. By the same token, in the United States, a nonwhite person who is second- or third-generation immigrant, even one with perfect command of the English language and no trace of a foreign accent is still asked what country he or she comes from. In contrast, whites of European descent are rapidly assimilated and pass for full-fledged Americans.

In America, racial or ethnic identification is pivotal in determining a person's relative status and chances for success. Statistical, demographic, and residential information predict educational achievement, income, school dropout and suspension rates, family size, mortality trends, incarceration rates, tendencies to violence, use of welfare, and other presumed dysfunctional characteristics that configurate the American justice system, investment and banking activities, and even distribution of resources and liabilities (from the location of banks, grocery stores, movie theaters to those of waste disposal, prisons, and nuclear sites). As Ladson-Billings and Tate (1995) have emphasized, social class and gender considerations alone "are not powerful enough to explain all the difference (or variance) in school experience and performance," consequently we must conclude that "race continues to be a significant factor in determining inequity in the United States" (pp. 48–49). Because elementary and secondary school performance are affected by race and ethnicity, the size and quality of pools of racially and ethnically different candidates for higher education positions are limited. Additionally, the racial and/or ethnic prejudice in the society at large is reflected not only in elementary and secondary public schools, but also in higher education institutions. And it extends to the most critical areas: the hiring, promotion, and retention norms and procedures.

In a broader historical perspective, the pendulum-like cycles of tolerance or intolerance for racial and ethnic diversity in the United States are often associated with military, socioeconomic, cultural, and political crises. These crises bring an intensity to the stereotyping, scapegoating, and persecuting of immigrants, rationalized as a legitimate concern for national security, crime prevention, the protection of our economic interests, or cultural purity.

A critical analysis of the history of immigrants in Europe and the United States should help us understand the reality of the hardships faced by all immigrants (see C. Suárez-Orozco & M. M. Suárez-Orozco, 1995; M. M. Suárez-Orozco, 1991). Indeed, we must go far beyond the romantic fantasies of America as the archetypal country of immigrants with an exemplary democracy, the land of opportunity for all, and the land of freedom. For America has also been the land of exploitation of the ignorant, the poor, and the needy; the land in which children of color are neglected, warehoused in awful places called "schools" placed under freeways or in unsafe ghettoes;

the land where young immigrant women still work in the most abject, unsanitary, and oppressive conditions in sweatshops, packing companies, or in agricultural fields where they are exposed to toxic pesticides from dawn to sunset as pickers, without health insurance and for a fraction of the salary earned by whites making less than the minimum salary (Trueba, 1996). The reality is that without the cheap labor of these immigrants, the wealth of the U.S. textile companies and agribusiness corporations would not exist. Many of these immigrants stay in this country for one reason: to help their children get a good education and a chance at a better life.

In his book entitled *Shadowed lives: Undocumented immigrants in American society* (a case study in a cultural anthropology collection edited by George and Louise Spindler), Leo Chavez (1992) cites a *New York Times* editorial of 1880:

> There is a limit to our power of assimilation. . . . [W]e are not in need of any more aliens at present. Foreigners who come here and herd together like sheep remain foreigners all their lives. We know how stubbornly conservative of his dirt and his ignorance is the average immigrant who settles in New York, particularly if he is of a clannish race like the Italians. Born in squalor, raised in filth and misery and kept at work almost from infancy, these wretched beings change their abode, but not their habits. . . . (p. 14)

The use of the words "race" and "clannish race" is indicative of the historical confusion between race and ethnicity. There is nothing new in the recent efforts to "close our borders" and do away with illegal immigration. Xenophobia is more subtle within university walls and has nothing comparable to the dramatic high-tech flamboyant cavalry of new immigration officers riding along the wall dividing Tijuana from San Diego. Nevertheless, when search and personnel committees meet to discuss candidates, the nativistic tendencies of white Americans of European ancestry come across loud and clear. Many immigrants do excel in school and eventually join universities; but they also continue to face difficulties as did other immigrants from the turn of the century until the mid-1920s who were accused of moral turpitude and socially ostracized only because they used their home language to communicate with each other and with some students.

Although immigration trends have changed drastically since the 1920s with the dramatic increase in Hispanic and Asian populations, the working conditions and exploitation of many immigrants has not changed. Throughout their lives, many immigrants (for example, farm workers in

California) work in fields at low wages and in unhealthy conditions because they want to improve their children's opportunities. Education is their best hope of getting out of poverty. In this context, racial and ethnic intolerance in higher education profoundly affects the access and quality of education for racial and ethnic minority students. An institution that is primarily created and maintained by white faculty will present perspectives and values that exclude, penalize, or ignore students of color. The consistent reluctance of higher education institutions to diversify its faculty is clearly impinging on the quality of education offered for all students. Even white students need to understand ethnically and racially diverse populations in this country. Their insulation from minorities perpetuates their prejudices and inabilities to deal with populations of color.

Perspectives on Race and Ethnicity in Higher Education

Judging from current sentiment in academia, one cannot assume that in the near future there will be serious change toward a fair representation of Latino and African American faculty in higher education, nor even a continuation of the efforts that followed the rhetoric of diversification the last two decades (Olivas, 1994, pp. 117–138). Most strategies adopted in the name of affirmative action, equity, curriculum reform, competitiveness in the college market for minority students, or for political expediency (to retain state or federal dollars), have failed to produced sustained gains in the numbers of tenured Latino or African American faculty. The outcomes have been disappointing. (1) In some institutions, there is the "revolving-door" syndrome (minority faculty were hired and left soon after). (2) In others, honest recruitment efforts were neutralized by aggressive opposition of white faculty and traditional gatekeeping mechanisms. In the end, minority candidates didn't meet the expected performance criteria required to be tenured and were "legitimately" rejected—without being counseled, mentored, assisted, supported, and taught to become productive intellectuals like white faculty. In other words, ethnically different faculty were placed in a rather hostile environment and simply dismissed.

Many of the writers in this book have first-hand experiences of gatekeeping and rejection. My first shock in this country came when I sought a job in a somewhat famous white institution. I had a very good record in graduate work, very strong letters of recommendation, and support from the faculty but in my first interview I was rejected by the dean of the college. He said publicly that he did not like my "Mexican" accent. My main professor, George Peter Murdock (an internationally renowned anthropologist) called that dean to give him a piece of his mind and helped me get an interview and a job in another institution the next day. I felt vindicated but insecure.

While advancing my career in academia as an administrator, I witnessed at close hand the political contortions white faculty used to rationalize their biases and the invocation of the sacred academic values, educational philosophy (read "cultural values"), academic freedom (read "white faculty control of academic processes"), and "harmony" (read "fear of brown, black, and other ethnics"). Personnel and search committees ready to veto a candidate of color may open the discussion with a calculated speech (often with an inflated and artificial air of solemnity) on the justification of preserving departmental quality and traditions. The commentary can be typified by the following:

> We are committed to academic excellence and equity at any cost. And we are equally committed to oppose political activism because it will destroy our solidarity and jeopardize the quality of our work. In principle, we open our door to all minority candidates, and we will treat them well, the same way we treat other candidates. However, we oppose any political action [read "affirmative action"] to favor one candidate over others. We cannot give any advantage to any racial or ethnic group, because that would violate senate policy and compromise our academic freedom. The candidates with the best academic record, those who meet our departmental needs, and best fit our institution [read "our white faculty"], will be given the position. (Summary of recollection and field notes)

This position will exclude any conscious systematic effort to attract racially and ethnically different faculty. The criteria to judge the qualities and suitability of a candidate are interpreted and applied by committees without ethnic representation because "homogeneous committees understand the needs and sentiments of departmental faculty," as a dean explained to me. But even departments that recognize the need for hiring faculty of color and don't object philosophically to searches for qualified candidates from specific ethnic and racial groups (especially searches for "targets of excellence" intended to bring persons with highest academic records), often raise serious questions about the appropriateness of minority searches. Such committees often ask:

> Are these searches compatible with our academic freedom? Are they an effective means of attracting African American, Latinos and other minorities? Why don't we let

the good candidates surface to the top during the search? What is the payoff, the expected benefits, and the ultimate goal of minority searches? But even we who assume that these searches make sense question if they can become effective without creating conflict and divisiveness in [the] university? (Summary of recollection and field notes)

Many faculty who consider themselves fair, democratic, and conscientious academics would like to know whether (1) the political contexts and circumstances under which these searches take place, do, in fact, render them unsuccessful; and whether (2) the short- and long-term strategies for recruiting minority faculty have adopted a new philosophy of education and have undergone other important changes. These questions are legitimate and deserve answers. I hope to offer at least some partial answers to these questions, using my own experience.

My Own Experience as a Faculty Member and an Administrator

I have worked in higher education since 1969. My first teaching and administrative job was as assistant professor and interim chair of the Anthropology/Sociology Department at Western Illinois University in a small town called Macomb. Subsequently, I taught briefly at California State University, Sacramento, and worked for a number of years at the University of Illinois at Champaign-Urbana. After this, I became departmental chair at San Diego State University for a short time, and in 1982 went to the University of California at Santa Barbara where I stayed for 8 years. From there I went to the University of California at Davis, the University of Wisconsin at Madison, and only recently to the University of Houston. I also was a visiting professor at the University of Alaska at Fairbanks, the University of Leuven in Belgium, Stanford, Michigan State, and most recently (during FY 1995–96) at UC-Santa Barbara. I have had short-term visits at many other institutions in Sweden, Spain, Brazil, and especially Mexico, where I was born and had spent 30 years of my life. I know the *universidades autónomas* system and the *tecnológicos* and had extended contacts with other universities and research centers in Tijuana, Ciudad Juárez, Monterrey, Mexicali, Querétaro, Puebla, and Mexico City. This broad experience across institutions in different countries has helped me notice the unique and persistent patterns of interethnic interaction in American universities.

Drawing on my 27 years of academic experience, I will describe the main challenges and dilemmas faculty and administrators face in their attempts to create a pluralistic and culturally diverse environment in higher education. I will also suggest additional strategies to pursue the goal of diversification. These strategies will be directed to increasing the size of the eligible minority pool and establishing fair and effective university policies and procedures to recruit, hire, and retain the best-qualified candidates from underrepresented ethnic and racial groups. I will select specific examples from institutions I know best: the University of California at Davis (where I was associate dean of Letters and Science and director of the Division of Education), the University of Wisconsin at Madison (where I was dean of the School of Education and where I worked closely with then Chancellor Donna Shalala), and the University of Houston (where I worked as the senior vice president for Academic Affairs and provost). I use these examples only to illustrate specific points without revealing names of persons or institutions.

Recent controversies about the meaning, philosophy, policy, and practice of affirmative action in the California higher education systems have revealed that there is not only a wide range of interpretations and positions about affirmative action, but also a profound discontent with the performance of higher education institutions. Indeed, these debates have reopened the question of how realistic and appropriate the California Master Plan is. At the very least, there is a need to redefine the goals of higher education in the context of savage budget cuts, decreasing public support, and lack of state resources. According to the media, the public is limiting the amount of resources going to universities because of the presumed overpolitization of the university's intellectual life and its focus on racial and ethnic conflicts. The assumption is that discourse on race and ethnicity is a disruptive factor in academia and compromises the quality of higher education institutions. These concerns are not new; they have been expressed in various academic communities over the past three decades in different forms and forums. There is a righteous tone among some academicians who claim they are protecting the purity of academia.

The academicians taking a purist approach emphasize the sanctity of the academic institution with all its traditions and practices and the significance of scholarly endeavors (research and instruction), which must be protected from the destructive politics of minority activists. Minority hiring and promotions are seen as the cause (some say the effect) of political activism in the university, which ultimately could destroy the excellence of an institution. For university administrators to tolerate political activism is nothing less than to preside over the demise of research institutions, to witness in silence their deterioration, and, in the end, to compromise the foundations of American democracy. In the minds of some, diversification is the number-one enemy of social harmony, scientific and technical development, and democracy.

This stance of maintaining the racial and ethnic status quo in academia carries a number of contradictions and dilemmas, even for righteous academicians. Learning and teaching are political, and literacy education is cultural action for liberation, according to the position defended by Freire (1973, 1993) and many of his followers, especially critical theorists and sociologists of education (see Apple, 1978, 1982, 1985, 1989, 1990, 1992, 1993; Aronowitz & Giroux, 1985, 1991; Giroux, 1983, 1992; Giroux & McLaren, 1986, 1994; McLaren, 1995; McLaren & Leonard, 1993). Yet, in the United States, some academicians view political action, on the one hand, as dysfunctional, irreverent, unacceptable, and ultimately deplorable. They are concerned that our universities may turn into political arenas (as happened in Mexico and Latin America, where political turmoil often caused disorder and prevented instruction and research). Never mind that in American institutions there are few instances of faculty even questioning publicly white hegemonic control of the hiring, promoting, and tenuring processes. On the other hand, political action by white faculty to resist changes in these processes is seen as perfectly all right, or even admirable and necessary.

Why is it so disturbing for white faculty to hire and retain African American or Latino faculty? The discomfort that the mere thought of diversification brings to some is a basic fear of the unknown; it is a profound discomfort that comes with uncertainty about how diversification will affect white life-style and their control of educational institutions. Fear of change is not necessarily racism. Organized resistance to change can also be motivated by racism or fear of discomfort. Ultimately, permitting change toward diversification in higher education can mean losing power to control the institutional resources, status, and benefits that come with a faculty position. Losing power also means losing comfort. To secure some measure of comfort, white faculty develop unusual abilities to rationalize their politics of tacit reluctance to attract or retain faculty of color. They may argue that:

1. "The candidate does not have the qualifications required for the job."
2. "The candidate could not adjust to the modus operandi and traditions of the institution."
3. "The position is not good for the candidate; he or she won't be happy in the company of whites."
4. "The students will not like and will not learn with people of color; worse still, students may destroy the candidate."

Specific Cases and Some Reflections

Despite the opposition, some candidates of color manage to gain support and make their way to a short list and a final interview. When the process of selection is focused on a candidate of color whose qualifications are comparable to those of white candidates, a red light calls for "spontaneous" caucusing of the faculty in communication with the search committee, a period of deep anxiety, and intense political action. New inquiries are made into the candidate's qualifications and background. White faculty communicate with each other and debate. Political pressure requires that white faculty appear to be liberal, fair, open-minded, and concerned citizens, willing to "give a chance" to candidates of color. But what if the candidate of color turns out to be "antiwhite" and difficult, yet academically sound? The reactions of some faculty are then fear, confusion, and anger. The closer the possibility of hiring a person of color gets, the more vicious the arguments against the candidate become. I have several examples.

A Chicana in a Research Institution

This case involved a Chicana (a female Mexican American) who came from a low-income family (farm workers from Mexico). She came to the United States when she was 10 years old, after having had very irregular schooling. Her teachers discovered her intelligence and mentored her to leave home and go to college. The Chicana went to Stanford and obtained her doctorate. After two years of part-time employment and a postdoctoral fellowship, she made her way to a final interview for a tenure-track position in a research institution. Her qualifications and performance were acceptable and, compared to the other candidates, superior. The search committee was divided along ethnic lines. The faculty discussed the candidate in the halls, cafeteria, and offices. A departmental meeting was called to assess faculty reaction after her formal lecture and visit. The negative comments began immediately: "She could not teach here"; "She is a self-deprecating Chicana who does not know how to finish a sentence"; "Her research is marginal"; "We don't want any trouble with ethnic groups. . . ."

The tacit hostility during the interview did not bother the Chicana, who had moved up from poverty to earn a doctorate from Stanford University. Since trying to finish high school to go to college, through her admission interview at Stanford, but especially after her major adviser abandoned her at the point of dissertation, she decided she would succeed at any cost. The chair of her dissertation committee, a famous woman researcher, had no tolerance for drafts with any typographical errors. After noticing a few mistakes in the first eight pages, she picked up the dissertation draft and threw it in the wastepaper basket in disgust. Normally, when students bring their first drafts, the committee chair goes over the entire manuscript primarily for content and organization in order to check the main ideas, the conceptual framework, the findings, and conclusions. After the major organizational issues are cleared, the chair recommends a careful checking of the entire text for syntax, punctuation, correct spelling, format, and other details. The gesture of throwing away somebody's dissertation is inappropriate and insulting. If the chair was angry and wanted to make the point that she demanded a perfect draft, she could have returned the draft saying, "When you correct this draft, I will be happy to read it." As the Chicana's peers often stated, this student was a trooper and had "muchos huevos" ("lots of guts," as Mexicans say). She completed the dissertation, received her Ph.D., and was proud of her achievements.

It might be thought that opportunities for teaching and research positions would open up everywhere. The reality was that it was even difficult to get an interview. And when this interview took place at a major research university, it was a major event, and somewhat traumatic. At the departmental meeting, the secretaries counted the votes cast by the faculty and passed the results to me. I realized that several full professors who had not attended the Chicana's lecture had commented negatively about her presentation. It was obvious that several full professors had cast negative votes without even meeting this Chicana. In addition, two or three anonymous letters were sent to the search committee that I had the opportunity to read. The tone of the letters was violent and the attacks vicious; her appearance, work, speech —everything was targeted. I recognized the handwriting in one of the letters and confronted the professor in question. He was embarrassed and tried to justify why he wanted to prevent the Chicana from being hired. He admitted that he had never spoken to her directly but had relied on the testimony of his colleagues. The search committee negotiated an extra position with the vice chancellor and hired this woman. She has done extremely well and now has the respect of her colleagues.

A Dean's Search

There was a search for dean of a college. The pool of candidates was very large and competitive. The college was extremely political and factionalized. The search committee proposed a short list with an African American candidate, a white woman, and two white men. After a series of controversial faculty meetings, and for a number of complex procedural and political reasons (for example, the white male faculty caucused and questioned the African American candidate's credentials), the original support given to the African American as one of the finalists decreased. An offer was made to a white male, who turned it down. The search was closed and an inside member of the faculty was appointed dean. During the conflict between the various factions, there were a great number of attacks from one group or faculty against the others, and there were letters with vicious remarks directed at particular members of ethnic groups (against a Hispanic and two Jewish faculty members). The passion and almost hatred among professors was a shock to me.

Hispanics Singled Out

In a small college that had had fiscal and personnel problems, an inside white member of the faculty was appointed dean. This new dean had earlier expressed his misgivings about the quality of a Hispanic woman who entered the college as "a target of opportunity hire." Gradually, for a number of personal reasons, the dean decided to remove this woman and a Hispanic male from their tenure-track positions.

During the third probationary year, assistant professors can be let go if there is evidence of underperformance or other strong reasons. From the first year on, it was clear that the dean wanted to remove these two faculty members from the college. To obtain support from the administration to remove them, he declared "financial exigency" on the grounds that the previous year's cuts had left the college without funds to keep all assistant professors. Financial exigency was not an appropriate action for the dean to take since the budget cut was so small; normally, the central administration would negotiate ways of absorbing the budget cut.

The dean requested approval to transfer the two Hispanic faculty to temporary positions immediately, so as to terminate them the following year. The Hispanic male was already nationally recognized as an extremely talented individual, well published and committed to scholarship. The faculty resisted the move against him. The Hispanic woman had less support among the faculy. Convinced that the dean was unfair and biased, she threatened to sue. She contacted the Office of Civil Rights, and the pressure finally persuaded the dean to give up the idea of an early transfer from a tenure-track to a temporary position. This woman was devastated and demoralized to the point that she could not function effectively for several months. She agreed to stop her civil rights inquiry when her status was clarified as tenure track.

Not Hiring and Retaining Outstanding Latino Faculty

The dean of a very large college, who was generally liked by Latinos, learned that several departments had identified (through regular searches) two Latino women of high caliber. The internal struggles in those departments made it "politically risky" to support the best candidates (the Latino women) found by the search committee. The dean decided not to hire anybody and thus avoided displeasing one of the groups, white senior faculty.

The same dean knew about an award-winning Latino associate professor who was the author of an outstanding book in his field. This professor was underpaid and had received a number of invitations to visit other campuses that wanted to hire him. There were several mechanisms that the dean could have used in order to retain this faculty member (for example, offer a salary increase, a chair, support in terms of new resources, public recognition ceremonies, and so on, or a combination of the above). The dean did not talk about any of these possibilities with the chair of the department, and the associate professor began to look elsewhere for a position. Fortunately, a group of Latino faculty gave him advice and support and persuaded him to stay. This Latino faculty member is now demoralized and, if his wife can find a job elsewhere, he is willing to move.

Why would a dean who has the funds and opportunity to hire and/or keep outstanding Latino candidates give in to the pressure of senior faculty? Obviously, the dean does not have the stature and courage to do what is right and defend the quality of a department.

Power of the Chair and of the Faculty
in Rejecting Latinos

Another case involved a Latino male with an international reputation as a scholar and researcher. He was extremely productive—a person who wrote in five different languages and maintained a publication record that was extraordinary. He was also considered one of the best in his field and, at the time of this incident, was teaching in a very prestigious institution. An invitation to bring the top five final candidates reached my desk, and I realized that the Latino professor was not among them. I requested the folders of all the finalists for the position from the department chair and the chair of the search committee and asked them to compare all the finalists with the Latino professor. I ended a long session with the committee chair and was persuaded that the committee could not find any valid reason to exclude the Latino professor; he just intimidated the white faculty. The main reason given for selecting the much weaker white candidates was that they suited departmental needs and had greater faculty support. Current faculty (some with publication records inferior to that of the Latino candidate) attacked the Latino candidate viciously.

This was a department with a history of rejecting other Latinos. At different times, two outstanding Latino candidates with doctorates from Stanford and strong letters of recommendation were invited to apply for positions and interviewed. These candidates should have been the highest ranking ones. Their visits were mishandled, the faculty was divided in their support, and some professors expressed concerns about the possible overlapping of their specializations in comparison with the existing faculty. Neither candidate was hired, and both ended in first-rate institutions (one at Harvard and the other at UCLA). In the same college, a junior Chicano faculty, with a doctorate from Stanford and a highly promising publication record, was hired as assistant professor. He was made chair of Chicano Studies and also received a heavy teaching load. His teaching evaluations were the highest ever in the department. However, his writing slowed down, and he became demoralized. He felt that nobody, especially senior faculty, ever made an effort to make him feel welcome or help him in any way. He resigned and took a position in a very competitive institution where he obtained tenure and renewed his publishing career.

An almost identical case occurred in the same department, except in this case the Chicano faculty member had spent six years hoping to be tenured, and, in the end, other faculty began to spread rumors that he was not going to receive it. He left and was hired with tenure in a highly prestigious university. His publications are well received, and he is the editor of an important journal in his field.

I could cite many more examples. These, however, are sufficient to make my point. In ways that are sometimes very subtle and other times very explicit and vicious, underrepresented minority persons are mistreated and rejected in higher education without reason and against all principles of equity and fairness. These examples are anonymous because it is not my purpose to point fingers at anybody or at any institution. I believe that in most of the cases I described, white faculty members felt justified in acting the way they did and had no guilty feelings or any sense of responsibility to assist, mentor, and help young minority faculty trying to succeed in competitive white academic institutions. But I also know that even the most outstanding white faculty often lack sensitivity about these issues.

In the final analysis, the "balancing act" for some white faculty consists of keeping academia "pure" by rejecting underrepresented minorities, but doing it without guilt or penalties (without lawsuits, loss of status and credibility, loss of federal funding, or public support). Perhaps this is done more subtly in research institutions that enjoy the status of having the highest academic standards but liberal and progressive thought. Being liberal and progressive does not mean that faculty of color are recruited for tenured positions or that the core of decision makers has become less white. In fact, some of these liberal institutions attract some minority faculty but keep very few; they have very strict retention criteria that either discourage faculty of color from applying or they bring candidates of color for a short time, only to screen them out periodically.

The treatment described above and other reasons explain why so few Hispanics and other minority persons are in tenured faculty ranks. First, the pipeline of well-trained, highly qualified racial and ethnic minority faculty is quite small. Second, who among them would want to pursue a career in those "liberal and progressive" institutions that offer a revolving-door option to most minority faculty? The pool of minority faculty is relatively small because (1) few have the minimum qualifications to enter doctoral programs; (2) the mentoring of doctoral students is deficient; and (3) these students' academic socialization is deficient, and they tend to become ignored or marginalized.

In my experiences in a number of institutions, and according to the testimony of many colleagues with whom I discussed this matter, white students are more frequently cultivated, guided, and supported because they know how to obtain support and exhibit the appropriate behaviors at every inch of the journey. This is so much the case that my Latino colleagues often exchange bizarre stories about their days in the doctoral program; tough days of anxiety, humiliation, and abandonment by an insensitive faculty who could not see the talent behind the color. For example, successful faculty, now teaching in various institutions, who came originally from Stanford in the 1980s, tell stories similar to the ones discussed above. In the end, they had to beg a kind, older faculty person to help them complete their dissertation because they did not feel they had enough support from their doctoral committee members. Here at Harvard, there are doctoral Latino students who left the University of California for those very reasons. They remember when their doctoral committee not only failed to guide them but did not even attempt to offer support when other faculty members attacked them.

We are always amazed that, in spite of many obstacles, students of color manage to finish and graduate. Faculty have little faith in their intellectual capacity and motivation, so they don't give them their time, don't share ideas with them, and don't ask them to participate in their projects. As discussed above, sometimes they even throw the first draft of a dissertation into the wastepaper basket. In other instances, they resign from doctoral committees at the last minute, or stay but show total disregard and lack or respect for these students' ideas and fields of interest. Having struggled to get the doctorate, a minority candidate for a position is not surprised by the abuse of white faculty, but is deeply offended and demoralized. I know many current faculty whose stories have been confirmed by other students of color. They see the hiring and promotion processes as a logical sequence to their treatment as minority doctoral students. Their wounds stay open a long time, and their scars never disappear.

Is it difficult to gatekeep and reject ethnic and racial minorities? It is not, and it happens often. Can be justified or rationalized? Yes. In the ultimate instance, resistance to incorporate underrepresented minorities into the rank and file of the faculty in higher education is justified by one or several of the following arguments:

1. Quality control considerations ("There are no qualified candidates, and we need to preserve the quality of our department in order to generate knowledge and compete well.")

2. The need to preserve academic freedom from the imposition of affirmative action hirings ("Our field has other needs, and we must be free to pursue the right candidates to meet such needs.")

3. The need to prevent ethnic conflict ("Hiring minorities will bring political activism and disorder; we must protect the harmony of our academic climate")

Quality control, academic freedom, and harmony would seem to be important attributes of research institutions and therefore deserving our commitment. If we analyze quality control considerations, we realize that the criteria of discerning quality are not applied with equity.

The starting faculty assumption is that candidates of color are of lower quality than white candidates; the resulting exclusion of people of color can lead to inbreeding, intellectual rigidity, and conceptual poverty. We deprive ourselves of views, opinions, talents, and options advocated by people with different cultural experiences. The enrichment and challenging intellectual exchanges taking place with diversified faculty cannot exist where uniformity and conformity are preferred over a rich variety of views and experiences. Universities are the intellectual arena par excellence for conceptual growth, creative thinking, and acquisition of specialized discourse and linguistic repertoires. Universities are, furthermore, the place for intensive reflection on acquired knowledge and the joint construction of new knowledge. In this arena, the significance and timeliness of contributions by thinkers with other cultural (ethnic, linguistic, and social) experiences are critical to the education of all. People of color are urgently needed in higher education institutions because they help prepare all students to face the real world, which is culturally diverse; indeed, faculty of color can be the most instrumental education in white institutions. The analytical skills, discourse patterns, and rich experience of faculty of color will transcend the taboos and cultural codes of white faculty in undiversified institutions. Without faculty of color, the academic experience of students is impoverished.

In the social and medical sciences, education, art, music, law, business administration, technology, and other fields, the contributions of researchers and professors of color is essential to the full understanding of the field as it changes vis-à-vis population changes in America, Europe, and other countries. The relevancy of cultural differences in those fields is at the essence of their growth and success. In the other fields, such as engineering, the natural sciences, mathematics, etc., a better understanding of cultural differences and sensitivity to such differences can mean success or failure in attracting international markets, outstanding talent, financial support, and ultimately a broad network of scholars and researchers involved in the field for the benefit of all. Academia is itself universal; restrictions based on race or ethnicity can only decrease any institution's potential to compete well nationally and internationally. Racial and ethnic biases are most destructive to the institution and its students in all fields.

Issues about Harmony and the Avoidance of Racial or Ethnic Conflict in the University

In America, democracy is supposed to serve as a model to other nations. In order for our universities to live up to democratic principles of equity (equal opportunity; fair treatment of all; equal access to knowledge, faculty, and resources), they must start by attracting individuals who, having the disciplinary—theoretical and methodological—qualifications, are also capable of understanding the racial and ethnic characteristics of students, community, and other populations affected by the university. To teach effectively, one needs to communicate effectively. Individuals who are competent in dealing with diverse ethnic and racial groups can best serve their pedagogical needs.

Strategies for Diversification

First, we have to face the fact that some academicians committed to high-quality instruction and research view affirmative action policies and practices, indeed, any extradepartmental hiring initiatives as intrinsically incompatible with academic freedom and doomed to fail. The fundamental assumption is that hiring is the quintessence of academic freedom and that imposing color as a required characteristic of a potential faculty may exclude the most talented and suitable individuals. The experiments in faculty diversification on a quick-time basis created the revolving-door phenomenon. Rather than forcing departments to hire or promote persons of color, I think that chairpersons, deans, and vice presidents for academic affairs must create positive incentives for diversification with long-term perspectives. Two important working assumptions of administrators are:

1. Retain as the primary criterion for hiring, the highest academic qualifications of the candidate, and his or her potential to bring about significant contributions to the field and the academic unit.
2. Conduct searches with equity for all candidates regardless of color, race, ethnicity, gender, and disability.

Positive incentives to attract volunteer white faculty into the diversification effort will help avoid the appearance of "forcing" faculty, "violating" their academic freedom, or infringing on their rights in any way. At times, and in some political contexts, positive incentives offered by administrators to departments, in the form of additional financial resources to hire minorities—with maximum flexibility to select their specialization, gender, ethnicity, and race—can be viewed as an infringement of academic freedom or as bribes to impose a direction considered detrimental to the overall quality of academia. It is a very delicate matter faced by administrators, who find themselves in the cross fire of opposite and conflicting factions. An administrator can persuade and encourage, but can not impose personnel decisions on departmental chairs, search committees, or faculty. Consequently, the only avenue open to an administrator is often indirect action somewhat detached from personnel decisions. This action can take different forms:

1. Financial resources and flexibility to use them; visibility, moral support, and recognition.

2. Help to department (or other units) to expand searches, negotiate joint positions and obtain additional resources to attract a candidate.

3. Negative sanctions imposed on units or factions that consistently and systematically organized to defeat qualified persons from ethnic/racial underrepresented groups. These sanctions can take the form of budgetary reduction or fiscal restrictions, denial of moral support, recognition, information, etc.

The best higher education institutions often consider themselves as the most liberal (or less biased against underrepresented groups). Yet, they may also be the ones with the least representation of diverse ethnic and racial groups in tenured positions, that is, with the fewest African American and Latino tenured faculty. In these institutions, there are less conspicuous efforts to block the entrance of qualified candidates. The reluctance to tenure African American and Latino may be based on a deep commitment by all faculty to keep "their" standards of academic excellence and their conviction that most members of minority groups do not possess the necessary qualifications. As a result, and given the composition of most hiring committees, that is, mainstream persons with their particular social networks, it is often very difficult to attract a sufficient number of African American or Latino candidates with records comparable to those of mainstream candidates. This makes the job of hiring committees rather difficult, even when these committees show some willingness to consider a wide range of candidates.

The exclusion of underrepresented groups may be more the result of myopia and insensitivity than of organized racism. If we accept the above assumptions, and in good faith accept the willingness of some institutions to oppose engineered racism or exclusion (that is, reject overt political pressure to ignore, neglect, reject, and fail potential faculty from underrepresented ethnical or racial groups), then we must create the mechanism to enlarge the pool of candidates and socialize them into success. Having accepted these assumptions, academicians (administrators and faculty) must explore creative mechanisms to resolve the fundamental challenge of expanding the pools of candidates from underrepresented groups.

Specific Recommendations and Conclusion

Expanding the pool is only a necessary condition, not a sufficient one, for successful hiring, promotion, and retention of persons from underrepresented racial and ethnic groups. Additional strategies must address the serious problem of mentoring, guiding, developing, and nurturing minority faculty so they become genuine, active, and vital participants in academia. To accomplish these two goals, I propose the establishment of what I will call University Centers of Excellence (UCEs) in prestigious universities. Through a combination of partnerships with and grants from federal, state, and private organizations, as well as with the investment of private donations and revenues from services and publications from the UCEs, selected universities could sponsor further training and specialization of doctoral candidates (at the dissertation level), and of recent graduates as postdoctoral fellows in disciplinary fields of the greatest need and in fields lacking faculty from underrepresented groups. The organization and functions of the UCEs could be as follows:

1. Under the leadership of key university administrators, a group of mentors, ideally senior and highly recognized scholars, would use a portion of their time to conduct joint research and teaching activities with specific UCE members.

2. Mentoring of UCE members should be extended to their participation in seminars, conferences, and research projects across institutions.

3. A central part of the experience of UCE members would consist of an intense socialization in conducting research and writing, in acquiring additional methodological and analytical skills, in developing networks with peers and senior scholars, and in exploring interdisciplinary approaches to the study of socioeconomic, educational, and political problems of minority achievement.

4. The UCEs would offer members with continuous guidance, administrative internships, and rich academic experiences and multiple contacts in order to identify adequate tenure-track positions in universities where their professional growth is considered a top priority.

5. UCEs would hold annual conferences and bring back alumni who would help place and nurture UCE members.

Ultimately, the UCEs would create adequate networks and support systems to help potential faculty from underrepresented groups find adequate positions and ensure their intellectual and professional maximum development. In conclusion, the time has come to invest seriously, consistently, and substantially in intellectual and material resources to create a strong pool of underrepresented minority faculty who can take university positions in administration, research, and instruction and can demonstrate a level of performance above that of mainstream faculty. This can be done if we plan carefully the processes of academic socialization in order to select, support, and mentor the new faculty. The social and intellectual significance of a movement toward minority excellence is bound to have an impact at all levels of education and would give this country the momentum to continue to live up to its ideal as a democratic society.

NOTE

1. Portions of this chapter will appear in a forthcoming volume by Enrique T. Trueba, *Latinos unidos: Ethnic solidarity in linguistic, cultural and social diversity*, published by Rowman & Littlefield.

REFERENCES

Apple, M. (1978). The new sociology of education: Analyzing cultural and economic reproduction. *Harvard Educational Review, 48*, 495–503.

Apple, M. (1982). *Cultural and economic reproduction in education*. New York: Macmillan.

Apple, M. (1985) [1982]. *Education and power*. Boston: Ark Paperbacks.

Apple, M. (1989) [1986]. *Teachers & texts: A political economy of class & gender relations in education*. New York: Routledge.

Apple, M. (1990) [1979]. *Ideology and curriculum*. London: Routledge & Kegan Paul.

Apple, M. (1992). Do the standards go far enough? Power, policy, and practices in mathematics education. *Journal for Research in Mathematics Education, 23*(5), 412–431.

Apple, M. (1993). *Official knowledge: Democratic education in a conservative age*. New York and London: Routledge.

Aronowitz, S., & Giroux, H. A. (1985). *Education under siege*. South Hadley, MA: Bergin & Garvey.

Aronowitz, S., & Giroux, H. (1991). *Postmodern education: Politics, culture & social criticism*. Minneapolis: University of Minnesota Press.

Chavez, L. R. (1992). *Shadowed lives: Undocumented immigrants in American society*. In G. Spindler & L. Spindler (Eds.), *Case studies in cultural anthropology*. New York: Harcourt Brace Jovanovich.

Freire, P. (1973). *Pedagogy of the oppressed.* New York: Seabury.

Freire, P. (1993). *Pedagogia da Esperança: Um reencontro com a pedagogia do oprimido.* Sâo Paulo: Editora Paz e Terra, S.A.

Giroux, H. (1983). Theories of reproduction and resistance in the new sociology of education: A critical analysis. *Harvard Educational Review, 53*(3), 257–293.

Giroux, H. (1992). Educational leadership and the crisis of democratic government. *Educational Researcher, 21*(4), 4–11.

Giroux, H., & McLaren, P. (1986). Teacher education and the politics of engagement: The case for democratic schooling. *Harvard Educational Review, 26*(3), 213–238.

Giroux, H., & McLaren, P. (1994). *Between borders: Pedagogy and the politics of cultural studies.* New York and London: Routledge.

Ladson-Billings, G., & Tate, IV, W. (1995). Toward a critical race theory of education. *Teachers College Record, 97*(1), 47–68.

McLaren, P., & Leonard, P. (1993). *Paulo Freire: A critical encounter.* New York and London: Routledge.

McLaren, P. (1995). *Critical pedagogy and predatory culture.* New York and London: Routledge.

Olivas, M. (1994). Latinos and the law: An essay on crop cultivation. *UCLA Law Review, 14*, 117–138.

Suárez-Orozco, C., & Suárez-Orozco, M. M. (1995). *Transformation: Immigration, family life and achievement motivation among Latino adolescents.* Stanford: Stanford University Press.

Suárez-Orozco, M. M. (Ed.). (1991). Migration, minority status, and education: European dilemmas and responses in the 1990s [Special issue]. *Anthropology and Education Quarterly, 22*(2).

Trueba, H. T. (1996). *The study of a rural Mexican town.* Unpublished manuscript. University of California Linguistic Minority Research Institute. University of California, Santa Barbara.

Trueba, H. T., Jacobs, L., & Kirton, E. (1990). *Cultural conflict and adaptation: The case of the Hmong children in American society.* London: Falmer Press.

Trueba, H., Cheng, L., & Ima, K. (1993). *Myth or reality: Adaptive strategies of Asian Americans in California.* London: Falmer Press.

Trueba, H. T., Rodriguez, C., Zou, Y., & Cintrón, J. (1993). *Healing multicultural America: Mexican immigrants rise to power in rural California.* London: Falmer Press.

Trueba, H., & Zou, Y. (1994). *Power in education: The case of Miao university students and its significance for American culture.* London: Falmer Press.

Five Recommendations to Build a Multicultural Campus

Administrator—Vice President
Myrtis H. Powell

- Top management must *serve* its commitment to multiculturalism by having diverse representation on the senior administrative team.

- Student affairs must *train* their staff in valuing diversity as part of a quality plan for the executive level.

- The university/college must *obtain* quality information by using focus groups to discuss its strategic plan.

- The institution must *recognize* and *address* issues impacting students of color in the strategic plan, even if modifications are necessary.

- An enrollment management plan must be *designed* to recruit, retain, and graduate all students, especially students of color.

Five

Campus Climate and Students of Color

This chapter will address some effects of campus climate on the performance and experiences of students of color on traditional campuses. For purposes of this discussion, students of color include African Americans, Native Americans (including Alaskan Natives), Asian Americans, Pacific Islanders, and Hispanics (Latinos, Chicanos). I use the word "traditional" to refer to predominantly white four-year colleges and universities.

First, I review American higher education and its historic stance regarding the education of students of color, especially African Americans. Since African Americans have led the struggle for equality in higher education and paved the way for other underrepresented groups, their historic experiences are explored as a platform for the succeeding discussion.

Then I explore the academic so-called success of students of color on traditional campuses. I review the low enrollment, persistence, and graduation rates of students of color on traditional white campuses and present some ideas as to why "success rates," except for some Asian Americans, do not reflect their undergraduate enrollment.

I suggest an enrollment management program as a strategy to improve retention. Throughout the discussion, the importance of a positive campus environment for the success of students of color is woven. Campus climate receives special attention as one component of an enrollment management program focused on retaining students of color. The components include: institutional research, orientation, academic advising, and campus climate issues.

The discussion ends in search of a multicultural campus, the challenge and roles of student affairs professionals. I propose a response to a question that W.E.B. DuBois posed in 1903, which I paraphrase as, "Is there still hope and faith in the ultimate justice of things?"

The Changing Landscape of Higher Education

Social, political, economic events, legal and legislative challenges, and more importantly, demographic shifts have forever changed the landscape of American higher education. Traditional white colleges and universities are becoming more diverse. In the early 1950s, 94% of all students were white. By 1991, more than one student in six was nonwhite.

Between 1973 and 1993, the enrollment of students of color on traditional white four-year campuses rose steadily. The number of African American and Hispanic students increased by 9% and 6%, respectively. In the decade between 1982 and 1993, enrollment for African American, Hispanic, Asian American, Native American, and Alaskan Native students mushroomed by 57.6%, though the latter make up less than 1% of college-enrolled students of color (Carter & Wilson, 1994). Total college enrollment declined by 1.2% between 1992 and 1993, caused by a 2.5% decrease in white enrollment. The total enrollment of African Americans increased by 1.3% in the same period, the smallest gain among the four major ethnic minority groups. Between 1990 and 1993, Hispanics and Asian Americans had the largest enrollment increase, with gains of 26.3% each.

The Rocky Road to Higher Education
for America's Minorities

Despite these gains, the legacy of American higher education's treatment of students of color is cause for shame. Its history is one of exclusion, segregation, and racism. Even after the 1954 Supreme Court decision, *Brown v. Board of Education of Topeka*, which declared separate but equal education illegal for African Americans and indirectly for all students of color, many traditional colleges and universities resisted opening their doors fully. Many fought bitterly and complied, reluctantly, only after state and federal courts intervened.

Even when a few students of color were grudgingly admitted, this was only the first of many barriers they had to overcome. They were often subjected to physical and psychological indignities, segregated and inferior housing and dining facilities, restricted access to classes and curriculum, and generally hostile campus living and learning environments. Students of color, particularly African Americans, have steadfastly maintained their quest for equality in higher learning despite the determination of their reluctant suitors, white colleges and universities, to deny them this privilege. These academic battlefields are the legacies of U.S. higher education. It is on the ashes of the racist past that traditional white institutions are attempting to build multicultural campuses.

It is important to review African Americans' historic quest for education in order to set the stage for learning how students of color, through forced illiteracy, arrived at this inequitable stage of higher education.

Separate and Unequal Education for African Americans

The gains by African Americans have, more often than not, been made in the face of powerful resistance, sometimes violent, intimidation, discrimination, indifference, and benign neglect. According to Ballard (1994[1973]),

> Nothing reveals the direct connection between American higher education and the operating principles of American society better than the record of white universities in regard to the black question over the 100 year span between Emancipation and the beginning of open admission efforts in the mid-1960s. There can be no charitable explanation for the almost total exclusion of Blacks from the faculties, student bodies, and curriculum of these colleges. Never can there be any justification for the role that the universities played in creating a scholarly rationale for the caste system that emerged over the past century. Little can be gained by punishing the white educational structure for its past actions, but the extent to which the American university tradition was an active ally in the national policy of repression of African American people should be made absolutely clear. (p. 39)

It has been estimated that at the beginning of the Civil War, less than 5% of southern African Americans (4.5 million slaves and .5 million free persons) could be called somewhat literate. Two contradictions framed the debate regarding education of African Americans. The first asked whether they had the capacity for learning, particularly higher learning. The second was an attempt to deny them the opportunity to learn. Hence, at the time of Emancipation, there were laws against educating African Americans in every southern state. Even so, Horace Bond (1934) paints a dramatic picture of their thirst for knowledge once the order of freedom was given:

> At no time or place in America has there been exemplified so pathetic a faith in education as the lever of racial progress. Grown men studied their alphabet in the fields, holding the "blue-back speller" with one hand while they guided the plow with the other. Mothers tramped scores of miles to towns where they could place their children in school. Pine torches illuminated the dirt floored cabins where men, women and children studied until far into the night. No mass movement has been more in the American tradition than the urge which drove Negroes toward education soon after the Civil War. (p. 23)

The first African Americans graduated from white Bowdin college in 1826 and from Amherst in the same year. By 1954, less than 1% (4,080) of 480,000 freshmen students entering white colleges and universities were African American. (Ballard, 1994[1973]). During this period of forced segregation by traditional white colleges and universities, African Americans participated in higher learning in large numbers by establishing and enrolling in Black colleges and schools. A combination of self-help and the zeal of northern white abolitionists and missionaries had established schools and colleges for African Americans to combat the education apartheid system in America. After the Civil War, federal government and private philanthropic initiatives supported these early efforts and began new ones to educate former slaves. Historically Black colleges and universities (HBCUs) trace their heritage to those early movements.

The significance of these colleges in the education of African Americans cannot be overstated. Prior to the middle of 1960, they assumed the major responsibility for preparing the African American population for participation in the economic, social, and political worlds of the United States. In 1989, 8 of the 10 higher education institutions that awarded the most African American baccalaureate degrees were public HBCUs. Twenty-eight percent of all African Americans attending four-year institutions were enrolled in HBCUs in 1992, where 27.6% of all baccalaureate degrees earned by African Americans were awarded (Carter & Wilson, 1994).

The doors of traditional all-white educational institutions are legally open to all. Black colleges, however, are still the only hope for many aspiring African American high school graduates. Black colleges still provide, without apology, remedial preparation to students who come underprepared for the rigors of a college education. Many of these colleges are major competitors for top African American students. And many of these top students choose traditional black colleges because they find them more hospitable, caring, and nurturing.

Success Matters, and How Well Are Students of Color Doing on Traditional White Campuses?

By all barometers used to measure success in higher education, students of color, except for Asian Americans, are not doing well. African Americans and Hispanics continue to trail whites in college participation. Nearly 42% of white high school graduates 18–24 years old were enrolled in college in 1993, compared to 32.9% for African Americans and 35.8% for Hispanics. The dropout rate for minority students, particularly African Americans is unacceptably high. The percentage of baccalaureate degrees earned by students of color at traditional four-year campuses is disproportionately lower than their undergraduate enrollments.

Traditional campuses have paid more attention to recruiting and admitting students of color and much less attention to retaining them. Many of these students have special needs that require attention. Others come well prepared, enthusiastic, and self-directed, only to become dispirited, discouraged, and angry. Too often, these students suffer academically because of the way they experience their college environments.

Retention involves keeping students enrolled to completion of their objectives (Dolence, Miyahari, Grajeda, & Rapp, 1987–88). The goal is to maintain continuous enrollment and educational progress to graduation. The usual expectation for students who enter a four-year college immediately after graduation from high school has been that they will graduate within four years. Those who persist are defined by Ottinger (1991) as students who enter college immediately after high school graduation, maintain continuous enrollment for four years, and graduate by the end of the fourth regular academic year. The graduation rates for those who persist are determined by those students who receive the baccalaureate degree within six years.

Information on enrollment and graduation rates distilled from the 1995 American Council on Education report (Carter, 1995) is shown in Tables 1, 2, and 3 below.

Table 1 shows that there has been a 14.3% increase in the number of students enrolled in all four-year institutions between 1982 and 1993. White enrollment had the lowest increase (5.3%), followed by that of African Americans (32.5%). The numbers for Hispanics, Asian Americans, and Native Americans increased by 88.6, 122.3, and 51.3% respectively, for an overall increase of 61.3% for all students of color.

TABLE 1

Total Enrollment at Four-Year Institutions in 1982–1993;
Percent Change from 1982–93 and 1992–93 by Race/Ethnicity
(Numbers in Thousands)

	1982	1992	1993	Percent Change 1982–93	Percent Change 1992–93
All	7,648	8,764	8,740	14.3	−0.3
White	6,306	6,744	6,643	5.3	−1.5
African American	612	791	811	32.5	2.5
Hispanic	229	410	432	88.6	5.4
Asian American	193	407	429	122.3	5.3
Native American	39	55	59	51.3	6.6
All Minorities	1,073	1,663	1,731	61.3	4.1

SOURCE: Carter & Wilson, 1994.

Table 2 shows the total number of and percentage change in bachelor's degrees received from 1981–82. Again, African Americans trailed Hispanics, Asian Americans, and Native Americans but slightly outpaced white students.

Table 3 shows that the number of bachelor's degrees earned by students of color did not reflect the increase in numbers who enrolled in college over a comparable 10-year period. Again, African Americans showed the greatest disparity (13.3%).

These and other reports are consistent in their findings that, except for Asian American students, the majority of high school graduates do not enter college immediately, and the persistence and graduation rates for students of color, particularly African Americans, lag behind those of other students at traditional white campuses.

TABLE 2

Bachelor's Degrees by Race/Ethnicity, 1981–92;
Percent Change from 1981 to 92 and Between
1981 and 1992 (Numbers in Thousands)

	1981	1992	Percent Change 1981–92	Percent Change 1991–92
All	934,800	1,129,883	20.9	4.5
White	807,319	936,771	16.0	3.6
African American	60,673	72,326	19.2	10.7
Hispanic	21,832	40,761	86.7	11.3
Asian American	18,794	46,720	148.6	12.3
Native American	3,593	5,176	44.1	14.7
All Minorities	1,104,892	164,983	57.3	11.4

SOURCE: Carter & Wilson, 1994.

TABLE 3

Comparison of Percentage of Enrollment Change Between 1981 and 1992
and Percent Change in Degrees Earned, 1982–92
(Numbers in Thousands)

	Percent Change in Enrollment 1982–93	Percent Change in Degrees Earned 1981–92
All	14.3	20.9
White	5.3	16.0
African American	32.5	19.2
Hispanic	88.6	86.7
Asian American	122.3	148.6
Native American	51.3	44.1
All Minorities	61.3	57.3

SOURCE: Carter & Wilson, 1994.

Keeping students of color enrolled at traditional white institutions is the most difficult part of a strategy to build a multicultural campus. Yet, unless colleges and universities retain and graduate these students, they will continue to play the replacement game, marching in place rather than progressing. It is estimated that it costs the average college or university approximately $1,200 to enroll one student (recruitment, publications, application review and processing, programming, etc.). It is easy to calculate the financial inefficiency in high attrition rates. The costs in human suffering to victims are incalculable.

Why Do Students Leave?

Numerous reasons are given as to why students of color leave predominantly white schools before graduation. Clewell and Fickle (1986) suggest that race and socioeconomic status, academic, personal, and financial difficulties cause many to leave. Ottinger (1991) believes that socioeconomic status affects persistence when ability is taken into account.

Mow and Nettles (1990) state that because of the small number of students of color on most traditional white college campuses and the considerable cultural and social adjustments they must make, researchers give little attention to the relationship between their experiences, performance, and persistence. Crosson (1988) cites negative racial climate as a factor in achievement of students of color. Getzlaf, Sedlacek, Kearney, and Blackwell (1984) found that the lack of educational preparation may make some students of color feel out of place on college campuses and drop out. Tinto (1975, 1986, 1987, 1990) suggests that retention is influenced by the degree of integration into the campus culture, which is determined by the levels of incongruence and isolation the student of color experiences. Malaney and Shively (1995) emphasize the importance of studying each racial minority group separately on individual campuses, since they found that different groups experience and react to their campus environments differently.

The reasons students of color drop out of predominantly white colleges and universities are complex and multifaceted. They include personal, social, academic and financial difficulties; language barriers; low self-esteem; fear and isolation; lack of family support; lack of experience with higher education; racism; discrimination; a misfit between the institution and the student; the one-size-fits-all approach to serving different populations by colleges and universities; lack of role models, mentors, and satisfactory peer relationships; faculty indifference and low expectations; and a general tendency of institutions to resist change. There is general agreement that for students of color, a welcoming, nurturing, and caring climate is crucial for retention; that student experiences during the freshman year on campus greatly influence their decision to stay or leave; and that a retention strategy to enhance the retention of students is imperative.

Student retention on many college campuses is often left to chance. Strategies to keep students of color and help them achieve personal, social, and academic success to graduation, where they exist, are often fragmented and unfocused. Predictably, results have been less than stellar, and there is a great deal of frustration and wasted resources. The shattered lives of hopeful students are the ultimate costs.

The challenges facing colleges and universities that are committed to the success of all admitted students require much more than minor adjustments. Not only must recruitment and admissions activities be broadened and made more strategic, but they must be integrated into a comprehensive campus-wide transformation that views education as a continuum from recruitment to graduation and beyond.

Enrollment Management: The Long Road from Recruitment to Graduation

The most promising strategy is an integrated enrollment management program. Williams (1993) reported that very few enrollment officers had comprehensive, integrated enrollment programs. While 94% had responsibility for admissions, only 89% were responsible for recruitment. Forty-seven percent were responsible for financial aid, and 35% had responsibility for retention. Although 57% had an active admissions or enrollment committee, only 57% of these committees had responsibility for issues relating to retention.

Hossler (1984) defined enrollment management as:

> a process or an activity, that influences the size, the shape, and the characteristics of a student body by directing institutional efforts in marketing, recruitment, and admissions as well as pricing and financial aid. In addition, the process exerts considerable influence on academic advising, institutional research agenda, orientation, retention studies, and student services. It is not simply an administrative process. Enrollment management involves the entire campus. (pp. 5–6)

Williams (1993) expanded Hossler's definition of enrollment by including institutional mission, organizational structure, resource allocation, and instruction.

Enrollment management is a comprehensive, integrated program designed to enhance recruitment, admission, matriculation, retention, and graduation. It doesn't require all related functions to be directed by the chief enrollment or admission officer or be the responsibility of student affairs. It demands a clear mission, articulated by the president and the president's cabinet. It requires planning, leadership, coordination and teamwork, and acknowledgment by the entire campus community that all members are stakeholders. It is a proactive, dynamic process that requires, at the outset, an evaluation component to measure effectiveness, resolve to discard activities that are not working, and flexibility to take corrective action as needed.

Five components of an integrated management program will be discussed: the enrollment management team (EMT); institutional research; orientation; academic advising; and campus climate.

The Enrollment Management Team

An enrollment management team (EMT) should include representation from the various units of the university—faculty, staff, administrators, and students from academic affairs, alumni, and development to operations and institutional research. Student participation is important since enrolled students can provide invaluable information beginning with their first contact with the institution and their experiences on campus. Someone has to be in charge. A leader or coordinator of the EMT should be designated.

The EMT should begin with a careful analysis of all units involved with recruitment, enrollment, and retention of students of color. The purpose and effectiveness of the disparate units should be assessed. It is important that commitments and input from these units be assured. Included in this analysis should be a review of the human and financial resources available to each unit. Pooling of these resources can be very important to a successful minority enrollment management strategy for students of color and lead to more effective use of scarce resources and avoid duplication of efforts.

Institutional Research

Accurate and timely information is key to a successful student of color enrollment management program. The EMT will need information about the institution's image (how it is viewed by students of color, parents, alumni, high school counselors, and others). An environmental scan, demographic analysis, experiences of students of color, campus ecology, retention and graduation statistics, postgraduate education, and job placement rates are all important data needed to develop a comprehensive enrollment management planning strategy and for setting realistic and achievable goals.

Orientation Program

Orientation is the first plank in an enrollment management plan. It assists the student in "joining up" with the institution. It is designed to acquaint students with the mission, culture, traditions, policies and procedures, rules and regulations, and services of the college or university. It is also the first opportunity for new students to interact and become acquainted with faculty, staff, and other students. The missions of the orientation program, according to the Council on the Advancement of Standards (CAS, 1986), is to "aid new students in their transition to the institution; expose new students to the broad educational opportunities of the institution; and integrate new students into the life of the institution." (p. 97) The goal is to help entering students adjust to their new environment and provide tools that will contribute to their personal development, growth, and academic success.

Comprehensive orientation programs provide students and parents with information on academic resources and expectations, including the "how to's" of course selection, registration, and scheduling; logistical information on how to negotiate the campus bureaucracy (business, financial aid and personal finances, tuition and fees, campus identification, and other campus resources such as books and academic and personal supply purchases); student support services, programs, activities, clubs and organizations; diagnostic tests for academic planning, placement, and career guidance; and transitional programs, including cultural diversity, male-female relationships, roommate complaints, substance abuse, and acquaintance rape (to name a few). Workshops for students and parents on separation fears, anxieties, and coping strategies are common. At Miami, an important part of the orientation program focuses on academic expectations and includes mini-lectures by professors.

A comprehensive orientation program also recognizes the needs of special populations and individual students. Adjustments and adaptations are made accordingly. Subsessions should be planned to acquaint special populations with culture-specific programs and activities. Some students of color and others may have inadequate preparation in one or more courses, which places them at risk of academic failure. Time should be set aside during orientation for diagnostic testing, assessment, and advising so that appropriate educational plans and strategies may be planned with them.

Students of color should be encouraged to attend the sessions designed for all students, as well as the special orientation sessions. Some students of color may not appreciate the importance of orientation sessions, may find the cost of attending prohibitive, or may find that attendance competes with summer employment. Special communications may be necessary to impress on these students and their parents the importance of these programs. Since academic advising, class selection, and registration are completed during these sessions, students who don't attend may find classes scarce if they wait until they arrive on campus. At Miami, we take into consideration the fact that,since the number of admitted students of color is often small compared to the number of other students, the number of students of color attending each orientation session will be small. One or two students of color in a group of two to three hundred white students can become "lost in the sea of whiteness." One way to avoid such an occurrence is to purposely designate one or more sessions to which groups of students of color are specifically invited. Those who attend have the opportunity to meet other entering students of color and facilitate the scheduling of special sessions as well.

Orientation programs vary in length from one- or two-day sessions to a week or longer. Workshops, seminars, or classes may be held for several weeks. The more successful ones are extended and may last the entire freshman year. Orientation is a campus activity involving students, faculty, administrators, and staff. What happens during orientation sets the tone for how students of color view the institution. It should show a commitment to the students' success. More importantly, orientation is the first step of a retention program.

Academic Advising

Academic advising is a second key strategy of a comprehensive enrollment management plan. It is a process that continues from orientation to graduation. Viewed narrowly, the function of academic advising is to provide information to the student on courses and schedules. It is prescriptive, "a relationship acknowledging the authority of the adviser and the limitation of the student." (Frost, 1991, p. 15) In this process, the student is a passive receptacle into which advisers deposit answers to questions asked by students about the tools of education (courses, registration, and schedules). Effective academic advising, according to Crookston (1972), is student centered, is a teaching process that addresses broad-based academic and intellectual concerns, and is a shared responsibility between student and teacher. Frost (1991) concurs that the academic process is a shared responsibility between student and adviser that involves problem solving and goal setting and explores careers and majors. The details of selecting and scheduling courses follow the broad exploration of options through a collaborative process between adviser and student. Effective academic advising helps students plan, take charge of their academic and personal lives, make a commitment to and invest in their college communities, and increase satisfaction. Satisfied students perform better and stay longer.

In 1986, the Council for the Advancement of Standards (CAS) published standards and guidelines for student services and development programs, including academic advising. These guidelines stated that,

> The primary purpose of an academic advising program is to assist students in the development of meaningful educational plans . . . compatible with their life goals. Academic advising should be viewed as a continuous process of clarification and evaluation. The ultimate responsibility for making decisions about life goals and educational plans rests with the individual student. The academic adviser assists by helping to identify and assess alternatives and the consequences of the decisions. (p. 11)

Inadequate academic advising programs can be detrimental for all students. But for those who must tread the unfamiliar and sometimes unfriendly terrain on traditional white college campuses, the outcome can be devastating and may cause students to drop out. Academic advising targeted to students of color can assist them in their social adjustment, intellectual development, and personal and academic success. Effective advising strategies targeted at students of color have six characteristics in common.

First, they are student centered and goal directed. The academic process begins before the first meeting with the adviser. The adviser must be familiar with the student's background and any special needs that may require intervention. The adviser must be familiar with the cultural backgrounds of students assigned to them. The advising relationship begins from a knowledge base instead of stereotypes.

Second, faculty are leaders in the academic advising process. Long ago, academic advising was the responsibility of faculty. However, today it is more and more frequently relegated to student affairs staff and professional advisers. While staff can be important adjuncts to a successful academic advising program, an academic advising program without faculty leadership is deficient. Research consistently points out the efficacy of frequent and meaningful student-faculty interaction in increasing student involvement and motivation. (Astin, 1984; Frost, 1991; Lang & Ford, 1992; Pascarella, 1980, 1985a, 1985b).

At Miami University, faculty responsibility for academic advising is part of the academic culture. Faculty members are an integral part of the orientation program. Academic advisers reside in residence halls with first-year students. Though these advisers are full-time student affairs staff members, they are trained by faculty members and are part of a council of academic advisers made up of staff and faculty from each academic division. In the middle of the second semester, students are assigned faculty advisers in academic departments who will follow them to graduation. In addition, each college and school has a full-time faculty or staff member whose primary responsibility is to act as advocate, mentor, and personal adviser to students of color, particularly African American students, the largest racial minority group on campus. These advocates are important liaisons with and between faculty and students and an important part of our enrollment management and retention programs for students of color. Students of color are also invited to participate in a mentor program where faculty and staff volunteer as mentors and friends, or where upper-class students of color "adopt" a new student.

A major problem at Miami is encouraging students to use the advising services available to them. Many students fail to do so until they experience academic problems. Also, too often both students of color and white faculty are reluctant to engage each other in more than discussions about course requirements, and the like. One program at Miami, now in its third year, is the Scholastic Enhancement Program. Of the 115–125 students assigned to it each year, about one-third are students of color. Each is assessed at the time of admission as having one or more risk factors that might prevent academic success. These students sign an agreement to meet once per week with the Scholastic Enhancement Adviser, at least during their first year. Failure to do so is cause to deny registration for subsequent semesters. Early indicators are that this is a powerful retention tool.

Third, advising targeted toward students of color is a "community affair." It is part of a broad retention effort and an academic priority. It is supported by the Board of Trustees, is an imperative of the president and other campus leaders, and has the commitment of faculty, staff, and students. At Miami, the process begins when students of color arrive on campus one day before other students, are welcomed with their families at a university picnic, meet with advisers and advocates, and get to know faculty, staff, and upper-class students.

Fourth, academic advising programs for students of color are transforming. Activities are designed to remove existing environmental barriers and negative on-campus experiences of minority students. Students of color are not required to reinvent themselves in the image of the college. They do not have to discard their individual cultures and heritages to "fit" the institution, but different cultures are valued, affirmed, and celebrated as being important to the diversity of the institutions. The institution changes to meet the success needs of all students.

Fifth, academic advising focused on students of color incorporates an appropriate balance between self-direction and prescriptive or intrusive interventions based on particular needs.

Sixth, faculty and staff of color are involved, but white faculty are equal partners in the program.

The academic advising program for students of color is focused on success. Advisers set high expectations for the students and empower them to achieve success. The program builds on the students' strengths, not on deficits. Where academic risk factors are identified, they aren't used to denigrate an individual, but as challenges to be overcome by the adviser and the student. Academic advising targeted to students of color on traditional campuses should be one part of a network of support services designed to help students stay in college to completion. It focuses on the well-being of the whole student—their academic, social, physical, career, and moral needs.

Academic advisers are trained, knowledgeable, and positive. They are teachers, mentors, counselors, and friends. This network has a coordinator, results are evaluated, and measures of accountability are built in. Recognizing and affirming the achievement of students of color is also very important. Miami University awards certificates and specially designed pins each semester to students of color who achieve a 3.2 grade point average and above. They are given these certificates and pins at a special dinner to which parents, faculty, staff, and student mentors are invited and at which the president addresses them. Again, this is part of our overall academic advising and retention strategy.

Improving Campus Environments

No retention plan for students of color can be successful if the environment on campus drives students away. A campus environment that is inhospitable to students of color is not healthy for any student. Improving the campus climate is perhaps the most important plank in any enrollment management strategy. The challenge is to create campus environments that reflect the cultural heterogeneity within and create a learning community where all students are treated with respect and helped to succeed.

Students of color often arrive on traditional campuses unprepared for the harsh realities they find. Many come from segregated schools where they are the majority. Overwhelming "whiteness" may cause a kind of culture shock. Many traditional white campuses have been intent on increasing their numbers without changing the campus climate. Many of these same campuses have paid little attention to how students of color perceive and experience their campus environments. Students of color are expected to fit in and negotiate their own way. It is naive to expect that just putting diverse people together will achieve some magical accord. Discord is often the result.

It is not easy to transcend our parochial past. These are frightening times, as campus leaders try to find common ground amid chaos. There is resistance to change within the academy. Campus discord reflects the national scene, which is characterized by talk show hosts who peddle hate and hatefulness, the shrill rhetoric of public officials, the dismantling of affirmative action, reductions in federal financial aid, attacks against scholarships designated to assist some special populations, and exclusionary legislation such as California's Proposition 187. All of these have created tensions on college campuses. The message is that it is all right to voice racial resentment—and many are doing so with a vengeance. Students spew hatred and hide behind the First Amendment. Faculty are resentful and question whether scarce resources should be spent on diversity efforts, whether multiculturalism is "central" to the mission and goals of the institution, and whether "standards" are being compromised. Some are uncomfortable with diverse groups, or apathetic or insensitive to their needs. The classroom climate is at best chilly and sometimes outright hostile, and when students of color protest, faculty hide behind the veil of academic freedom.

Students of color often feel that white faculty, staff, and students regard them as being less prepared, less deserving, affirmative-action quotas. Many experience open hostility, racism, discrimination, and isolation. Racial incidents on college campuses all across the country occur all too frequently. Though not all discrimination is overt, it is painful and harmful nonetheless. Students' reactions to treatment they receive are often misunderstood and result in further isolation and rejection. Consequently, students of color often withdraw into protective racial and ethnic conclaves. The dominant culture interprets this withdrawal as separatism, while students of color maintain it is basically a gathering of like minds. Such gatherings may serve as comfort zones or opportunities to learn about each other, or to resolve tensions within and between groups.

Once students of color arrive on a traditional campus, they become aware quite quickly through symbols, traditions, and activities that they have entered a place not built for them. They find that most activities do not reflect the full diversity of the campus. Multicultural activities and programs, where they do exist, are peripheral to the core campus culture. It is no wonder these students feel marginalized and estranged from such campuses.

Some institutions lack the conscience or the courage to acknowledge that something is wrong. Others respond timidly or move from crisis to crisis. A few are trying honestly to find order among the discord and are exasperated when their efforts seem to be unappreciated or not acknowledged. The response is often, "We spend lots of dollars on this issue. What do 'they' want from us?" Too often they fail to recognize that creating and managing diversity is hard work. It is a process that is dynamic, complex, unsettling, and often not very pretty. Because campuses literally renew themselves each year when new students arrive on campus, they can and should keep changing, adapting, and transforming. Green (1989) reminds us that changing the campus climate is central to the retention of students, faculty, and staff of color.

> Campus climate embraces the culture, habits, decisions, practices, and policies that make up campus life. It is the sum total of the daily environment, and centered to the "comfort factor" that minority students, faculty and staff, and administrators experience on campus. Students and other members of the campus who feel unwelcome or alienated from the mainstream of campus life are unlikely to remain. If they do remain, they are unlikely to be successful. . . . Changing the campus climate can be a difficult and illusive task. But, because the climate is so central to all other efforts to improve minority participation, it is both the point of departure and the culmination of all efforts. (p. 113)

To those who expect a smooth sail, hear Manning and Coleman-Boatwright (1991) describe the process of creating a multicultural environment as:

> steep 90° angles that community members must scale. The plateaus are not flat but can be viewed metaphorically like the rolling deck of a ship: slippery, difficult to traverse, and often treacherous. Hard won movement along this continuum is hard to sustain. The all-pervasive presence of the dominant culture in the organizational structure works against progress toward multiculturalism. The realities are not causes for discouragement but, rather, sources of understanding about the need for empowerment, policy making and goal advancement. The process must be rooted in long-term organizational development to achieve multiculturalism. (p. 371)

Student affairs professionals must understand the changes that are taking place and help the campus community scale the steep 90° angles inherent in responding to the cultural, social, and psychological needs of students of color.

In Search of Multiculturalism: The Challenges for Student Affairs Professionals

The ultimate challenge for student affairs professionals is to help create a multicultural campus. Student affairs professionals must become leaders and change agents in this search. They must act as both catalysts and facilitators, as helpers and prodders; they must both influence and help shape the multicultural campus. A multicultural campus is one on which members are purposefully diverse; communication is open, sensitive, and supportive of the different cultures; interaction is promoted between and among its diverse groups; and part of its mission includes embracing, valuing, and celebrating the achievements, talents, and uniqueness of all of its members.

Too often, attending to diversity and multicultural issues on traditional campuses has been the sole purview of student affairs staff while the rest of the campus continued business as usual. Student affairs cannot transform their campus alone and cannot meet the needs of all students. Student affairs staff have the distinct advantage, however, of knowing more about students than others on campus (or at least they should know more), therefore they have an obligation and opportunity to share what they know, see, and experience in their work with individuals and groups of students. Student affairs must know the background and needs of the various groups on campus, communicate these needs to the campus community, while advocating an appropriate response on behalf of students. The greater campus community must learn that all African American students are not disadvantaged; that they don't all know each other, speak alike, and think alike; that they all have not had the same life experiences; that no one African American student should be expected to speak for their entire race. And finally, they should know that the needs of African American females and males may differ significantly. The same is true for other ethnic groups, that is, Hispanics, Native Americans, etc.

Student affairs professionals must know that history, customs, and rituals of Native Americans may differ significantly according to one's tribe; that not all live on reservations and some have no history of living on them; that tribal sovereignty is important to preserving the cultural heritage of Native Americans. Finally, they must avoid speaking, reacting to, and dealing with Native Americans as though they are some exotic relic of the past. Native American peoples and their cultures are alive, present, and looking to the future.

Likewise, Asian Americans are not "Orientals," whatever that means. The diversity in this group is often overlooked since data are not usually collected or broken down by ethnic groups, citizenship, or length of residence in the United States. The Asian American population is made up of immigrants from China, the Philippines, Japan, India, Korea, Vietnam, Cambodia, Laos, and many other countries. Finally, student affairs professionals must learn and inform their campuses that although Asian Americans seem to be slightly overrepresented in higher education in proportion to their enrollment, there are significant disparities in the college enrollment, persistence, and graduation rates among the subgroups, as well as cultural, social, economic and language differences.

Campuses should be reminded that Hispanics are the fastest-growing minority group in the United States and are expected to be the largest population of people of color by 2010. Like other people of color, there is no monolithic Hispanic. This group includes Mexican Americans, Cubans, Puerto Ricans, and immigrants from Central and South America. Again, there are social, economic, educational, and language differences between the groups. Student affairs should have the most accurate lens on the diversity in the campus community and help the campus understand what is required to create a true multicultural community.

In addition to the multicultural diversity (ethnicity and color) of the new generation of students born between 1977 and 1993, there are other characteristics with profound implications for colleges and universities that must educate them. According to Susan Mitchell (1995), 72 million Americans were born during this 16-year period. Twenty-eight percent of them are 18 years of age or younger. The first of this group entered college in 1995 and will populate college and university campuses during the first decade of the twenty-first century. The original baby boomers were a relatively homogenous group. The new cohorts are not only more diverse racially and ethnically, but many are of mixed races, 34% are people of color, and only 67% are white. In 1964, only 64% of American births were white.

Although this new generation is more diverse, it is not likely that they will be more tolerant of each other. Indeed, they will likely be more polarized due to living in segregated neighborhoods and attending segregated schools; being exposed to more visible hate groups and more race-related violence; and having first-hand experience with integration, prejudice, and racial tensions between groups. The living and family arrangements of these students are also different. In 1970, 12% of students lived with one parent, and only 7% of those single parents had never been married. By 1993, 27% of students lived with one parent, and 31% of these single parents had never been married. Moreover, many more students will live in poverty, with extreme social differences in the rate of poverty between African Americans and whites. These first students of Mitchell's "new baby boom" entered our doors in September 1995. And these are the students who make it urgent that we create a multicultural community.

The Roles

In order for student affairs staff to assume leadership roles in helping institutions create multicultural communities, wise and committed leadership must come from the top. The responsibility is a shared one, and the entire campus must be involved. But student affairs staff cannot always wait for top leadership or faculty members to step forth.

- Student affairs professionals should model change, promote change, and reach out and encourage others to join in the change process.

- Student affairs professionals must bridge the divide between academic affairs and student affairs (perceived or real). Traditionally, the academic disciplines and curriculum were the faculty's domain. Student affairs staff were responsible for co-curricular and student development, services and activities and, generally, quality of campus life issues. Student affairs professionals must encourage the dismantling of these silos and create synergy between the two divisions. They must create partnerships with faculty and encourage meaningful collaborations for the well-being of minority and other students. They should first let faculty know what they know about students, by participating in new faculty orientation, by arranging forums to discuss minority student needs, providing feedback to faculty regarding what students say about climate in the classroom. Too often, when faculty act in inappropriate and hurtful ways, we concentrate on easing the pain and "fixing the immediate problem." But if we don't find ways to inform administrators and faculty about what is happening, no change takes place and the vicious cycle continues. Student affairs staff can share financial resources with faculty, who often must use their personal resources to engage students outside the classroom. They can also find ways to publicly thank and recognize faculty who step out and involve themselves in creating a just community. Finally, student affairs can be involved in planning activities which connect classroom and co-curricular learning, especially on residential campuses.

- Student affairs staff must encourage and involve student leaders in creating multicultural campuses. The staff must provide opportunities for students of color and white students to interact and increase understanding. White students must become part of the solution, not the problem.

- They must encourage and facilitate difficult dialogue between and within different student groups. Enabling students to discuss issues of concern to them, however discomforting, can help to reduce misunderstandings.

- They must find meaningful ways to involve parents and families in the academic and social lives of students of color.

- Student affairs staff must encourage and help students to plan and develop population specific programs and activities, participate and encourage white students and faculty to join in. Doing so can help reduce the use of stereotypes and reduce the discomfort and fear of difference.

- Student affairs staff must cultivate pluralism in cultural activities and student services.

- Student affairs staff must advocate, support, reinforce, and empower students of color to find their "place to be" on campus. They must not join the refrain of detractors who disdain such congregating as "segregating."

- Student affairs staff must involve faculty and staff of color in activities and programs for students of color.

- They must encourage ethnically diverse and white faculty to become mentors to students of color.

- They must empower students of color to take charge of their academic and social lives.

- They must set high expectations, expect success and concentrate on strengths, and help students to overcome shortcomings.

- They must provide multicultural training for student affairs staff, students, and others.

• And because it is inevitable that occasionally there will be open conflict, there should be in place dispute resolution mechanisms as well as policies for reporting and responding to bias-motivated incidents.

Is There Reason For Hope?

If student affairs professionals are to help build true multicultural campuses that incorporate the ideals of Boyer's (1990) purposeful, open, just, disciplined, caring, and celebrative community, they must lead by example. The task is not easy and knows no end. But with commitment, perseverance, and working together, there can be excitement, fulfillment and hope amid turbulence and chaos for all people in the twenty-first century, and perhaps higher education can help to redeem its checkered past. We must keep the faith in the struggle for cultural pluralism, human dignity, and the success of students. W.E.B. DuBois, in 1903, spoke of this faith:

> Through all the sorrow of the Sorrow Songs there breathes a hope—a faith in the ultimate justice of things. The minor cadences of despair change often to triumphs and calm confidence. Sometimes it is faith in life, sometimes a faith in death, sometimes assurance of boundless justice in some fair world beyond. But whichever it is, somehow men will judge men by their souls, and not by their skins. Is such hope justified? Do the Sorrow Songs sing true? (pp. 261–262)

The response to DuBois's question must be a resounding yes.

REFERENCES

Adelman, C. (1995). The new college course map and transcript files: Change in course-taking and achievement, 1972–1993. National Institute on Post-Secondary Education, Libraries and Lifelong Learning. Washington, DC: U.S. Department of Education.

Astin, A. W. (1984). Student involvement: A development theory for higher education. *Journal of College Student Personnel, 25,* 297–308.

Ballard, A. B. (1994). Academia's record of benign neglect. *Change,* p. 39. [Adapted from Ballard, A. B. (1973). *The education of Black folk: The Afro-American struggle for knowledge in white America.* New York: Harper and Row.]

Bond, H. M. (1934). *The education of the Negro in the American social order.* New York: Prentice-Hall

Boyer, E. L. (1990). *Campus life: In search of community.* Princeton: Carnegie Foundation for the Advancement of Teaching.

Carter, D. J. (1995). *Thirteenth annual status report on minorities in higher education.* Washington, DC: American Council on Education.

Carter, D. J., & Wilson, R. (1994). *Twelfth annual status report on minorities in higher education.* Washington, DC: American Council on Education.

Clewell, B. C., & Fickle, M. S. (1986). *Improving minority retention in higher education: A search for effective institutional practices.* Princeton: Educational Testing Service.

Council for the Advancement of Standards for Student Services/Development and Program. (1986). CAS Standards and Guidelines for Student Support Services/Development Programs. Washington, DC.

Crookston, B. B. (1972). A developmental view of academic advising as teaching. *Journal of College Student Personnel, 13,* 12–17.

Crosson, P. H. (1988). Four-year college and university environments for minority degree achievement. *Review of Higher Education, 11,* 305–382.

Dolence, M. G., Miyahari, D. H., Grajeda, J., & Rapp, C. (1987–88). Strategic enrollment management and planning. *Journal of the Society for College and University Planning, 16*(3), 55–74.

DuBois, W.E.B. (1903). *The souls of Black folk: Essays and sketches.* Chicago: A. C. McClury and Co.

Frost, S. H. (1991). *Academic advising for student success: A system of shared responsibility (ASHE-ERIC Higher Education Rep. No. 3).* Washington, DC: The George Washington University, School of Education and Human Development.

Getzlaf, S. B., Sedlacek, W. E., Kearney, C. P., & Blackwell, J. E. (1984). Two types of voluntary undergraduate attrition: An application of Tinto's model. *Research in Higher Education, 20,* 259–268.

Green, M. F. (1989). *Minorities on campus: A handbook for enhancing diversity.* Washington, DC: American Council on Education.

Hossler, D. (1984). *Enrollment management: An integrated approach.* New York: College Entrance Examination Board.

Hossler, D., & Bean, J. P. (1990). *The strategic management of college enrollments.* San Francisco: Jossey-Bass.

Lang, J., and Ford, C. A. (1992). *Strategies for retaining minority students in higher education.* Springfield, IL: Charles C. Thomas.

Malaney, G. D., & Shively, M. (1995). Academic and social expectation of first-year students of color. *NASPA Journal, 33,* 3–18.

Manning, K., & Coleman-Boatwright, P. (1991). Student affairs initiatives toward a multicultural university. *Journal of College Student Development, 32,* 367–374.

Mitchell, S. (1995). The next baby boom. *American Demographics, 17,* 22–31.

Mow, S. L., & Nettles, J. T. (1990). Minority student access to and persistence in college: A review of the trends and referral literature. In J. C. Smart (Ed.), *Higher education: Handbook of theory and research,* vol. 5 (pp. 35–105). New York: Agathon Press.

Ottinger, C. (1991). College-going persistence and completion patterns in higher education: What do we know? *Research Briefs, 2*(3). Division of Policy Analysis and Research. Washington, DC: American Council on Education.

Pascarella, E. T. (1980). Student, faculty informal contact and college outcomes. *Review of Educational Research, 4,* 545–595.

Pascarella, E. T. (1985a). College environmental influences on learning and cognitive development: A critical analysis and critique. In J. Smart (Ed.), *Higher education: Handbook of theory and research*, vol. 1. (pp. 1–61). New York: Agathon Press.

Pascarella, E. T. (1985b). Racial difference in factors associated with Bachelor's Degree completion: A nine year follow-up. *Research in Higher Education, 23,* 351–373.

Rhoads, R. A., & Black, M. A. (1995). Student affairs as transformational educators: Advancing a critical cultural perspective. *Journal of College Student Development, 36,* 413–420.

Tinto, V. (1975). Dropout from higher education: A theoretical synthesis of recent research. *Review of Educational Research, 45,* 89–125.

Tinto, V. (1986). Theories of student departure revisited. In J. C. Smart (Ed.), *Higher education: Handbook of theory and research*, vol. 2 (pp. 359–384). New York: Agathon.

Tinto, V. (1987). *Leaving college: Rethinking the causes and cures of student attrition.* Chicago: University of Chicago Press.

Tinto, V. (1990). Principles of effective retention. *Journal of Freshman Experiences, 2,* 35–48.

Williams, T. (1993). Enrollment management and financial aid: It is your job. *Admissions Marketing Report, 9*(4), 10–12.

PART III

Faculty Perspectives

Five Recommendations to Build a Multicultural Campus

Faculty
Flora Ida Ortiz

- The university/college must commit to promoting individuals *already* on the faculty.

- The entire hiring process must be *reviewed* to eliminate practices (for example, sponsorship or preferential treatment of friends) that impede faculty of color from appointment.

- Faculty of color must be *encouraged* and *supported* for developing new curriculum into the existing curriculum.

- Faculty of color must be *recruited* to work in all primary academic areas and not just ethnic or multicultural disciplines.

- Faculty of color must be *integrated* into the unit's existing network for mentoring and collaborative purposes.

Six

Career Patterns of People of Color
in Academia

This chapter deals with the issue of career patterns of people of color in academia. Two aspects are considered: (1) the positions available in academia; and (2) the individual movement within institutions. This report addresses the question: What is the interaction between the positions available in academia and the movement of people of color between those positions?

The latest report (U.S. Department of Education, 1995, p. 228) indicates that the total staff in institutions of higher education is comprised of 1,863,790 persons. The professional staff numbers 1,073,119. Nonfaculty professionals total 178,560 persons. The administrative ranks consist of 82,875 full-time males and 56,241 full-time females. The faculty consists of 366,213 full-time males and 169,410 full-time females. Given that dramatic demographic and social changes have taken place during the past three decades, what are the factors that contribute to the continuation of the dominance of white males in academia? Ordinarily, one would assume that a given academic institution would have positions similar to all other academic institutions, with the positions occupied by those who merit or openly compete for them, including people of color. However, that is not the case. Institutions differ in ethnic composition by types of institution. For example, community colleges are more likely to be comprised of people of color in greater numbers and in a greater variety of positions than all other types of academic institutions. Public four-year nonresearch universities are also more likely to have people of color in larger numbers and in a greater variety of positions than four-year doctoral and research universities. Public universities also appear to be friendlier to people of color than private universities, except for those universities explicitly instituted for a particular group of people, such as Black colleges.

Type of Academic Institution

Academic institutions differ in the types of programs they offer, the types of students they admit, the types of degrees they grant, and the types of expectations for their teaching staff. Community colleges typically offer two-year technical programs, remedial and preparation programs for four-year colleges, and programs that are appealing or necessary to an adult community. Admission to these institutions is open. A high school diploma or its equivalent is normally sufficient. Community colleges grant diplomas and/or certificates verifying the mastery of some technical skill or preparation for a four-year college. Their teaching staff are usually called instructors, and their work is generally totally consumed by teaching. Their careers are typically similar to those of high school teachers. Many instructors possess baccalaureate degrees. Some possess master's and a few have doctoral degrees. Typically, these instructors remain in their positions, receiving salary raises according to experience or as a result of obtaining a master's or doctoral degree. A few of them move to administrative posts within their discipline and may advance as deans or possibly become president of their institution or another community college. Both men and women of color attain presidencies of community colleges in greater numbers than in any other type of an academic institution.

Four-year public nonresearch academic institutions offer baccalaureate and master's degrees in a variety of programs. Admission requires that students rank in the top third of their class. Standardized test scores, letters of recommendation, and other evidence of ability and motivation are required for admission. Although research is encouraged, the heavy emphasis on teaching limits the amount of research possible for most faculty members. The careers of these faculty members are usually confined to the professorial ranks of assistant, associate, and full professor. A few faculty members become chair, assistant and associate professor, or dean as well as vice president, president, chancellor, or provost. Administrative positions may be obtained after directing large training and research special project programs. Having this experience in managing large budgets, personnel, and other resources, in addition to the wide-ranging contact and visibility, enables some faculty members to move to administration.

According to the Carnegie Commission on Higher Education (Fulton & Trow, 1974), which categorized institutions of higher learning as to both function and quality, 12.5% of 432,482 individuals with regular academic appointments in 1969 were in high-quality universities and 18.1% were in medium-quality universities. This means that between one-third and one-half of full-time faculty at the rank of instructor or above in four-year universities were subject to the rigid professorial academic norms associated with scholarly research and productivity. Burke's (1995) study shows that academic appointments and expectations are still similar to those reported by the Carnegie Commission on Higher Education.

The four-year research institutions are designed to offer doctoral programs and engage in research. Their students are drawn from the top 10–15% of high school student graduates. High grade-point averages, standardized test scores, letters of recommendation, and particular course requirements fulfill eligibility requirements for admission to these universities. The faculty teach reduced loads to enable them to conduct research and administer large research projects. In this type of institution, administrators are drawn from faculty if they have experience in administration of large budgets, personnel, and other resources as well as legitimacy in scholarly research.

Types of Positions People of Color Occupy

Persons of color enter these three institutions with differing ease, that is, community colleges are friendlier than four-year research universities. Almost all hiring in universities is at the lower ranks; openings at the level of associate or full professor are filled by promoting individuals already on the faculty (see Burke, 1995; Lewis, 1975; Logan, 1942).

An examination of the composition of these positions shows that 75.5% of full professors are white males and 14.3% are white females; 2.1% are African American males and 1.1% are African American females; 1.4% are Hispanic American males and 0.3% are Hispanic American females; 4.5% are Asian American males and 0.4% are Asian American females; and 0.2% are Native American males and 0.1% are Native American females.

In the associate professors rank, 63.1% are white males and 24.7% are white females; 2.9% are African American males and 2.1% are African American females; 1.3% are Hispanic American males and 0.8% are Hispanic American females; 3.6% are Asian American males and 1.0% are Asian American females; and 0.3% are Native American males and 0.1% are Native American females.

Finally, 47.5% of assistant professors are white males and 36% are white females; 2.8% are African American males and 3.0% are African American females; 2% are Hispanic American males and 1.2% are Hispanic American females; 5% are Asian American males and 2.1% are Asian American females; and 0.2% are Native American males and 0.2% are Native American females (Table 1 shows these distributions).

TABLE 1

Percentage of Professors in Universities by Gender and Ethnicity

Gender and Ethnicity	Full Professors	Associate Professors	Assistant Professors
	Percentage	Percentage	Percentage
White male	75.5	63.1	47.5
White female	14.3	24.7	36.0
Black male	2.1	2.9	2.8
Black female	1.1	2.1	3.0
Hispanic male	1.4	1.3	2.0
Hispanic female	0.3	0.8	1.2
Asian male	4.5	3.6	5.0
Asian female	0.4	1.0	2.1
Native American male	0.2	0.3	0.2
Native American female	0.1	0.1	0.2

Source: U.S. Department of Education, 1995.

The career pattern begins with the search, recruitment, and hiring of the new faculty member. The purpose of the search is to find the best person for the job. It is a very time-consuming task for faculty members who decide programmatic focus, rank, and composition of the search committee. Burke (1995) states, "There is a considerable amount of negotiation between chairs and deans before a position is authorized, but the *position definition* generally remains within the province of the academic department" (p. 8).

Three aspects to this activity remain important for applicants of color. First, once the "threshold of perceived ability is determined, the hiring process becomes closed and preferential rather than open and competitive" (Burke, 1995, p. 8). As the field narrows, the process of screening and selection focuses on ascription rather than achievement. Second, the letters of recommendation become pivotal documents that rely on the prestige of the writers. The issue for people of color is having contacts with those considered prestigious by the members of the search committee. Finally, the interview process may be the determining factor. Will the personal interaction between the recruiters and the person of color be an impressive one?

The appointment process assumes importance because, as Lewis (1975) reported, friends are the most frequent source of promising leads for positions. By phone, by letter, and in person, the recommendations preceding the candidate for the position facilitate the appointment process. Lewis found that those who teach in prestigious institutions are trained in prestigious institutions. Carrell (1968) likewise claimed that securing a good academic position is dependent on the prestige of the terminal degree and graduate sponsor. For people of color, social class is also an issue. Lewis wrote, "The system is less open than is generally acknowledged, and as a consequence the access of some individuals to the means of scientific and scholarly production is severely limited" (p. 146). All of these factors predispose people of color to be appointed to community colleges and to teaching positions in four-year institutions. Teaching, being viewed less positively than research and publication, predisposes academic institutions to grant a "place" to people of color in teaching positions. So, in the initial academic appointment the institution's action is to place a person of color in a position that emphasizes teaching.

Wilson (1989) wrote, "People of color whether faculty or administrators are commodified in ways their white counterparts are not . . . what often results is the positioning of faculty and administrators so that they have visibility (thus improving the institution's public image) but very little autonomy or power. Under these circumstances, people of color . . . are given place but not importance" (p. 12).

The place that Wilson is referring to is the appointment to the type of position in an institution. The Committee on College and University Teaching (1994) described academia this way, "Faculty workload combines teaching, scholarship, and service; this unity of components is meant to represent the seamless garment of academic life, and it defines the typical scholarly performance and career" (p. 46). Which positions are, then, likely to provide this career?

The prospective faculty member has two types of career decisions to make: the choice of discipline and the choice of academic setting. That is, will he or she choose sociology or chemistry at a community college, four-year university, or four-year research university? A place in the community college means teaching; in a four-year college, it means teaching and possibly research; in a four-year research university, the dominant focus is research.

Although the person of color may have chosen a traditional field such as sociology, the academic institution is likely to want to appoint him or her to an ethnic studies program or an area commonly linked with their ethnicity. An examination of academic institutions shows certain ethnic faculty concentrated in certain departments. For example, Aguirre and Martinez (1993) found Chicano faculty concentrated in Chicano or ethnic studies, Spanish, language, literature, and bilingual education departments. Some departments show an absence of certain groups. For example, Asian Americans are not likely to be in humanities, and African Americans and Hispanic Americans are not likely to be in engineering. These are consequences of appointment matches, "finding the best person for the job." Aguirre (1987) described this process as a channeling of Chicano faculty into a "limited opportunity structure in academe. This structure locates Chicano faculty in activities that may be quite visible, yet are peripheral to the mainstream activity in the post-secondary organization" (Aguirre & Martinez, 1993, p. 59).

The appointment process begins the career of the faculty of color. The rest of this chapter looks at the careers of faculty of color who are appointed to four-year research universities, with an emphasis on Chicano faculty. Recall that this is a very small number, because most people of color would be in community colleges and four-year nonresearch academic institutions.

The Establishment of an Academic Career

The modern academic career came of age by 1880, and the founding of the American Association of University Professors in 1915 served to professionalize it. By the end of World War II, the model of today was set:

teaching, research, student advisement, administration, and institutional and public service within the normative context of "professional autonomy, academic freedom, and universalism or the merit principle" (Carrell, 1968; Finkelstein, 1984, p. 141).

Schuster, Wheeler, & Associates (1990) identified four stages in a traditional academic career: (1) the novice professor, whose major concern is competence; (2) the early academic career when settling down, making a name, achieving, and confirming competence is focused on; (3) the midcareer, when a career plateau is accepted or new goals are set; and (4) the later career, when the concern is one of leaving a legacy. These stages are associated with the traditional advancement and promotion process in most universities. Obtaining tenure is proof that competence has been demonstrated, and the novice professor usually advances from assistant to associate professor at this time. Advancing to associate and full professor indicates achievement and confirms one's competence. Many professors, however, remain at the associate professor rank and never beome full professors. In other words, during the midcareer stage, many associate professors accept this plateau while others pursue advancement.

For people of color, movement through these stages is problematic. How the person combines teaching, research, and service determines the speed and height of advancement through academia. Their position in ethnic studies and as assistant professors will contribute to expectations that they teach and advise in undergraduate and large classes. They may also be less likely to receive funds for research than for training and program development. These characteristics may limit the ability to which a person of color can balance teaching, research, and service in order to advance in academia.

People of color are also expected to represent, speak, and act on behalf of their group. For example, Lopez and Schultz (1980) report that Chicano faculty are presumed to know everything about Chicanos simply because they are Chicano. However, this perception does not provide latitude for exercising authority in curricular matters. Instead, as Aguirre and Martinez (1993) report, Chicano faculty are used to "incorporate minor changes in the curriculum, but not to play a significant role in making decisions about academic policy." They could "propose course offerings in Chicano studies, but they could not use them to structure an academic major or program in Chicano studies" (Romero, 1977, p. 58). The small number of people of color in the institution may be exploited and restricted from participating in ways that promote academic success.

These practices may lead to stress arising from "placing excessive and incongruent demands on faculty" (Finklestein, 1984, pp. 142–143; Milem & Astin, 1993, p. 64).

These practices also contribute to isolation. Isolation results from containing faculty within their own ethnic group, thus, inhibiting them from developing necessary networks of support. By not being able to participate meaningfully in governance, they cannot develop networks that could alter the perceptions white faculty hold of them. They are denied the opportuniy to participate as department chairs, in personnel review committees, merit promotion committees, or tenure review committees (Aguirre, 1985; Arce, 1976; Escobedo, 1980; Milem & Astin, 1993).

Finally, invisibility affects their ability to identify with the university. As Aguirre and Martinez (1993) put it,

> one must keep in mind that Chicano faculty have embarked on "extraordinary careers" because they managed to transcend the social expectations ascribed to their minority status in U.S. society. . . . But academia treats them as strangers. In order to make the presence of people of color legitimate, the academic institution makes "sense" of their presence by supporting an opportunity structure that channels their participation to institutional sectors and activities focused on minority issues. (p. 63)

These "places" for people of color enable the institution to use the person of color to serve others like them and address the institution's need to offer an ethnically diverse curriculum (see Aguirre & Martinez, 1993; Padilla & Chavez Chavez, 1995). Such places, however, jeopardize academic success of people of color.

The most pronounced means of inhibiting people of color from advancing is the requirement of research and publication. Finkelstein (1984, p. 55) found that advancing in one's discipline through research was measured by three yardsticks: (1) receipt of honors and awards; (2) visibility of one's scholarly work to colleagues; and (3) actual use of one's scholarly work by colleagues.

All these factors are dependent on how an individual's research program can be controlled and conducted. Funded research makes a "special contribution to talented and dedicated faculty who, if all goes well, can move ahead as respected teacher-scholars within the academy" (p. 31). Funded research is more difficult for people of color to attain when they are not perceived as capable. Further, few universities "offer any training for project directors who must assume responsibility for implementing the numerous federal regulations relating to extramural monies" (Marshall, 1994, p. 31).

So, if people of color are perceived as unable to handle research, are too busy with other activities, and cover areas of research that are not valued by the academic community, how do they fulfill the requirement of research and publication? Many persons of color participate in research that deals with issues associated with their ethnic group or they compete for funds related to staff development and other programmatic areas. They use these forms of activities to generate research and publication.

Two aspects of this practice contribute to the success of people of color in academic institutions. First, the academic institution benefits from funds brought in by people of color. Second, the person of color gains visibility, knowledge, and skills related to administering budgets, personnel, and resources. Successful academic careers are indicated by: "career prestige and professional recognition, institutional monies for travel and conferences, opportunities to develop new course offerings or skills, salaries with stable purchasing power, and interinstitutional job mobility." These are all important "elements that support the successful negotiation of typical career transitions" (Schuster, Wheeler, & Associates, 1990, p. 125).

If the publication resulting from this activity will not be valued by the parent institution, the assistant professor has resources to move to another one and possibly as an administrator rather than a professor (Aguirre & Martinez, 1993; Garza, 1989).

Finkelstein (1984) identified three junctures at which academics may change jobs: (1) just before coming up for tenure; (2) just after promotion to full professor; and (3) just before coming up for promotion to full professor. Moving to administration at any one of these junctures is common, as is the practice to move from a four-year research university to administration in a four-year nonresearch university.

Many academicians of color believe that advancement under the regular conditions is almost impossible. Many of them fail to gain tenure and many of them leave academia altogether. Those who receive tenure, particularly males, associate themselves with projects related to their group such as staff development, bilingual education, or postdoctoral work for minorities. They manage large budgets, employ people, and mobilize to create visibility in their communities and elsewhere. If their campus remains aloof from these efforts, they seek to move to other campuses. When they move, they take their projects and advancements to their new campus. For example, an individual may move to a dean's position at another campus with their project.

Opportunities in Administration

Persons of color develop academic careers where movement from campus to campus with advancement is frequent. They are promoted through the professorial ranks, acquire administrative posts, and increase their salaries. Males, more commonly than females advance to the deanship. The process becomes more problematic as they seek positions of chancellor, provost, or president. The advancement may be to better and bigger and from public to private campuses.

The American Council of Education (ACE) (1994) report dealing with separate groups shows that in 1987, 328 women were chief executive officers of colleges and universities making up 11% of all presidents of approximately three thousand educational institutions. Forty-three or 1% of chief executive officers were women of color, 20 were African Americans, 16 were Hispanic Americans—most of whom head colleges in Puerto Rico—2 were Asian Americans, and 5 were Native American heads of so-called tribal colleges (see ACE, 1989; Farmer, 1993). In the same year, women of color held only 2% of all dean positions (College and University Personnel Association, 1994).

Movement in administration is reflected in a number of reports. Escueta and O'Brien (1995, p. 260) claim that 1 out of 100 executive managerial positions in higher education is held by an Asian American. This is contrasted with 1.1% of all administrative positions held by Asian Americans in 1983 (Wilson & Melendez, 1986). African Americans comprised 7.4% of administrators in higher education in 1979, decreasing to 6.8% in 1981, and increasing to 7.2% in 1983. In 1979, 1.4% of administrators were Hispanic Americans; in 1981 they comprised 1.7% (Wilson & Melendez, 1987; see Table 2). The underrepresentation of Latinos in university administration is shown in the sample of 18 administrative positions in the University of Texas and California in which only 2 positions were filled by Chicanos (Valverde, 1988). As indicated from the above, updated and specific figures regarding the representation of people of color in administrative positions in higher education are needed.

People of color may be tracked in administration. Wilson (1989) reported that women of color are "usually directors of remedial programs, affirmative action offices, and ethnic studies programs, positions which are not considered mainstream administration, and consequently, rarely lead to deanships, vice presidencies, or presidential positions no matter how talented the person happens to be" (p. 199).

TABLE 2
Administration by Year, Gender, and Ethnicity

Male	1979 %	1979 #	1981 %	1981 #	1983 %	1983 #	1987 %	1987 #	1988 %	1988 #
White	–	–	–	–	–	–	–	–	93	–
African American	7.4	–	6.8	–	7.2	–	–	–	–	100
Hispanic	1.4	–	1.7	–	–	–	–	–	–	37
Asian American	–	–	–	–	1.1	–	–	–	1.0	8
Native American	–	–	–	–	–	–	–	–	–	3

Female	1979 %	1979 #	1981 %	1981 #	1983 %	1983 #	1987 %	1987 #	1988 %	1988 #
White	–	–	–	–	–	–	–	–	9.5	200
African American	–	–	–	–	–	–	–	20	–	–
Hispanic	–	–	–	–	–	–	–	16	–	–
Asian American	–	–	–	–	–	–	–	2	–	–
Native American	–	–	–	–	–	–	–	5	–	–

Persons of color, as administrators, are held to many of the same expectations as when they were faculty members. Aguirre and Martinez (1993) report that Chicano administrators believe that "their credentials are more carefully scrutinized than those of Anglo administrators and are expected to perform at a higher level of competence than Anglo administrators in similar positions" (p. 58). Lopez and Schultz (1980) found that Chicano administrators are in implementation rather than policy-making roles. In other words, persons of color in administrative positions may not hold the degree of power and autonomy that is associated with the position. This restriction excludes them from attaining the top position of the institution.

Conclusions

People of color establish careers in academia in tracks that don't necessarily exclude them from the various positions. But they are restrained, and their work in each position tends to vary from that done by white males. First, people of color are tracked to community colleges and away from research and doctoral-granting institutions. Second, they are tracked to teaching and service and away from research, publication, and administration. Third, they are expected to represent and remain attached to their ethnic group as they occupy their position.

There are consequences to society, the institutions, and the individuals to tracking people of color in academia. Society is unable to benefit from the talents and knowledge of people of color. The institutions remain structured as always. And persons of color cannot fulfill their ambitions or display their skills and knowledge widely. In spite of restrictions, however, people of color are contributing to society, to the institutions, and to themselves. As these people of color occupy their positions, their presence benefits all; in fact, institutions do not hesitate to claim them. In addition to their very presence, their perspectives, skills, and knowledge are displayed as they practice their work. Those few who are engaged in teaching and administration need to acquire additional knowledge, engage in research, and publish. Confining people of color to teaching does not necessarily mean that they stop learning and producing knowledge.

As Padilla and Chavez Chavez (1995) wrote, "In order to face adversity of everyday life in academia, valuing the self becomes a necessity" (p. 10). This self-confidence enables people of color to train and sponsor students through instruction, research, and professional development. This collaboration calls for a complex system of producing new knowledge, preparing new academics, and providing an arena for administration. As people of color work together, they create networks among themselves, but may also break into networks of white males. As their movement from campus to campus increases and expands, the networks strengthen. Gonzales (1993) describes how she contributes to this strength. "I have found my voice, and I will speak what I know. What else can anybody offer me to beat that?" (p. 90).

This tracking system fragments and creates networks of "alikes" instead of integrating people of color within academia so that all parties can benefit from one other. For example, administrators may want to inhibit Chicano faculty from structuring an academic program in Chicano studies but may be willing to have them propose courses. The knowledge created and relayed remains contained, but it may strengthen the group in ways and degrees that can be crucial to all in the long run. What is important is that the production of knowledge does not stop by containing it. Instead, people of color are generating new knowledge and acquiring new skills and attitudes that are contributing to success. Since the practice of recruiting, hiring, and promoting is so strongly linked to friendship networks, reluctance to integrate people of color within the academic networks, does not mean that networks are not being created by people of color. What it does mean is that the creation of these networks is apart from and parallel to those of white males. These practices run counter to all of our beliefs regarding equity and meritocracy. Our question, then, is: Are these parallel systems of academic careers lodged on practices of discrimination?

Finkelstein (1984) presents three principal sources of evidence to test the thesis of overt discrimination: (1) studies of actual hiring decisions; (2) studies of discriminatory attitudes on the part of majority males; and (3) studies in inequity in the distribution of salary, promotion, and other rewards. From what has been previously presented, research in all of these three areas is notably absent.

This report shows how professors of color are expected to engage in teaching, research, and service in different proportions than white males. Because people of color hold the lower ranks of academic positions, their earnings are also lower than their white male counterparts. Moreover, Finkelstein (1984) found that "beyond teaching, research, and administration, women and minority faculty appear to be less involved in off-campus professional activities" (p. 199). Bowen and Schuster (1986) report that "half to three quarters of all faculty earn income for services rendered outside their institutions" (p. 28). This area of an academician's work remains to be examined.

The career patterns reported here persist even as dramatic changes are occurring in academia. The changes include the following: (1) The number of campuses has grown to nearly 3,400. The total number of faculty is about 710,000. (2) A broader strata of society is represented, with more people from modest family backgrounds, more women, and more members of people of color. (3) The faculty are more specialized, more rigorously educated, more worldly, and more experienced. (4) The proportion of part timers continues to rise: 35% in 1985 compared to 21.9% in 1970. *Nomads*, or gypsies (Schuster, Wheeler, & Associates, 1990) are persons on terminal contracts for a semester or two, a year or two, filling for faculty absent on leave. (5) The proportion of faculty employed in four-year colleges and universities continues to decrease; 70.4% in 1985 compared to 80.6% in 1970. And (6) there is a growing bipolarization of faculty, relatively young, and relatively old cohorts (Schuster, Wheeler, & Associates, 1990; U.S. Department of Education, 1987, pp. 158–159). If the present practices of tracking people of color continue, all of these changes mean that people of color may be the recipients of the most negative consequences.

REFERENCES

Aguirre, A. (1985). Chicano faculty at post-secondary educational institutions in the Southwest. *Journal of Educational Equity and Leadership, 5,* 133–144.

Aguirre, A. (1987). An interpretive analysis of Chicano faculty in academe. *Social Science Journal, 24,* 71–81.

Aguirre, A., & Martinez, R. O. (1993). *Chicanos in higher education: Issues and dilemmas for the 21st century.* Washington, DC: George Washington University.

American Council of Education (ACE). (1994). *Facts in brief: Higher education today.* Washington, DC: ACE.

American Council on Education, Office of Women in Higher Education (ACE). (1989). Typical college presidents: White, male, and married. *On Campus with Women, 18*(4), 8.

Arce, C. (1976). Chicanos in higher education. *Integrated Education, 14,* 14–18.

Bowen, H. R., & Schuster, J. H. (1986). *American professors: A national resource imperiled.* New York: Oxford University Press.

Burke, D. L. (1995). An academic workforce in transition. *Academe, 81,* 7–11.

Carrell, W. (1968). American college professors: 1750–1800. *History of Education Quarterly, 8,* 289–305.

Chavez Chavez, R., & Padilla, R. V. (1995). Introduction. In R. V. Padilla & R. Chavez Chavez (Eds.), *The leaning tower: Latino professors in American universities* (pp. 1–16). Albany: State University of New York Press.

College and University Personnel Association (CUPA). (1994). *1993–1994 National Faculty Salary Survey by Discipline and Rank in Private Colleges and Universities,* Washington, DC: Author.

Committee on College and University Teaching, Research and Publication (1994). Report: The work of faculty: Expectations, priorities and rewards. *Academe, 80,* 35–48.

Escobedo, T. (1980). Are Hispanic women in higher education the nonexistent minority? *Educational Researcher, 9,* 7–12.

Escueta, E., & O'Brien, E. (1995). Asian Americans in higher education: Trends and issues. In D. T. Nahanishi & T. Y. Nishida (Eds.), *The Asian American educational experience* (pp. 260–267). New York: Routledge.

Farmer, R. (1993). Place but not importance: The race for inclusion in academe. In J. Jones & R. Farmer (Eds.), *Spirit, space and survival: African American women in (white) academe* (pp. 199–202). New York: Routledge.

Finkelstein, M. J. (1984). *The American academic profession: A synthesis of social scientific inquiry since World War II.* Columbus: The Ohio State University Press.

Fulton, O. & Trow, M. (1974). Research activity in American higher education. *Sociology of Education, 47,* 34–47.

Garza, H. (1989). *Second class academics: Chicano/Latino faculty in U.S. universities.* Fresno: California State University Press.

Gonzales, M. C. (1995). In search of a voice I always had. In R. V. Padilla & R. Chavez Chavez (Eds.), *The leaning tower: Latino professors in American universities* (pp. 77–90). Albany: State University of New York Press.

Lewis, L. S. (1975). *Scaling the ivory tower: Merit and its limits in academic careers.* Baltimore: The Johns Hopkins University Press.

Logan, W. (1942). *The academic man.* New York: Oxford University Press.

Lopez, A., & Schultz, R. (1980). Role conflict of Chicano administrators in community colleges. *Community College Review, 7,* 50–55.

Marshall, R. (1994). Funded research and faculty time. *Academe, 80,* 30–31.

Milem, J., & Astin, H. (1993). The changing composition of the faculty: What does it really mean for diversity? *Change, 25,* 21–27.

Padilla, R. V., & Chavez Chavez, R. (1995). *The leaning tower: Latino professors in American universities.* Albany: State University of New York Press.

Romero, D. (1977, August). *The impact and use of minority faculty within a university.* Paper presented at the annual meeting of the American Psychological Association, San Francisco.

Schuster, J. H., Wheeler, D. W., & Associates. (1990). *Enhancing faculty careers: Strategies for development and renewal.* San Francisco: Jossey-Bass.

U.S. Department of Education. (1987). *Digest of education statistics.* Washington, DC: U.S. Government Printing Office.

U.S. Department of Education, Office of Educational Research and Improvement. (1995). *Digest of education statistics.* Washington, DC: U.S. Government Printing Office.

Valverde, L. (1988). The missing element: Hispanics at the top in higher education. *Change, 20,* 11.

Wilson, R. (1989). Women of color in acadmic administration: Trends, progress, and barriers *Sex Roles, 21*(1/2), 92–202.

Wilson, R., & Melendez, S. E. (1986). *Minorities in higher education: Fifth annual report.* Washington, DC: American Council on Education.

Wilson, R., & Melendez, S. E. (Eds.). (1987). *Sixth annual status report: Minorities in higher education.* Washington, DC: American Council on Education.

Five Recommendations to Build a Multicultural Campus

Faculty
A. Reynaldo Contreras

- Hispanic faculty must be *given opportunities* to play a significant role in making decisions about academic policy.

- The scholarship of Hispanic faculty must be *treated respectfully* as an integral component of the knowledge production of the unit.

- The local acculturation process for new faculty must be *reinvented* to accommodate Hispanic faculty.

- A *well-designed protégé-mentor program* is key to promoting academic success for Hispanic faculty.

- Hispanic faculty must *take advantage* of every opportunity to meet and socialize with significant stakeholders to garner "political capital" (for example, Board of Trustees, elected officials, and corporate leaders).

Seven

Leading from the Margins in the Ivory Tower

As Latino[1] populations continue to grow, it is expected that their enrollment in the educational system, especially institutions of higher education, will also increase, thereby further defining the multicultural academe. This increase in the enrollment of Latino students and other students of color in higher education will not only add to the cultural diversity of the student population, it will also pose significant challenges.

A significant challenge being given attention is the concept of "role models." Verdugo (1995) suggests that having role models means that individuals, representatives of a particular group, are in positions of status and power within and outside of institutions. In other words, these individuals have and are able to exercise institutional authority on behalf of organizational constituencies. The belief is that if students of color see other people of color in positions of authority and status exercising authority on their behalf, the students will not only be motivated to achieve and excel but will have a sounding board for the many problems they face in higher education.

Faculty of color are often targeted to fill this role. However, using faculty of color as role models has been limited or has failed because of the institutionally marginal status of nontraditional faculty in higher education. That is, faculty of color lack the institutional power and status that would enable them to fill such a role. In fact, those faculty of color who accessed higher education lead from the periphery of the academic institution, not only to survive but to break paths for other faculty of color and nontraditional students. A case in point is the Latino faculty.

This chapter has three purposes: (1) to illustrate how the Latino faculty is institutionally marginalized; (2) to examine the nature of leading from the margin; and (3) to suggest strategies for effective leadership from the periphery.

Latino Professorate in Higher Education

Presence

Verdugo (1995) observed that the total number of full-time Latino faculty in American higher education increased dramatically between 1979 and 1989. In this period, full-time Latino faculty increased by approximately 49%. This dramatic increase in the number of Latino faculty occurred at all ranks, but especially among full professors (Carter & Wilson, 1992).

However, Latino faculty are overrepresented at two-year institutions and underrepresented at four-year institutions (California State University, 1984; Committee on Education and Labor, 1984; Esquibel, 1977; Katsinas, 1984; Olivas, 1979; Valverde & Ramirez, 1977). In 1989, three times as many Latino faculty were employed at public two-year institutions (1.8%) as at public four-year institutions (0.6%) (Milem & Astin, 1993), but only 17% of Latino faculty were employed at four-year institutions (Uribe & Verdugo, 1990). While the concentration of Latino faculty at two-year institutions may reflect the enrollment pattern for Latino college students, the limited presence of Latino faculty at four-year institutions is more important because it means that Latino students in these institutions will have limited access to Latino faculty as role models and mentors (Verdugo, 1992). Latino faculty can play a crucial role in motivating Latino students to pursue graduate or professional degrees.

The underrepresentation of Latinos in the administrative structure in higher education institutions is even more acute than the underrepresentation of Latino faculty. For example, of 108 executive positions in the university system of Texas and California, only 2 were filled by Latinos (Valverde, 1988). And although one might assume that the concentration of Latino faculty at two-year institutions would make available a larger pool of Latino candidates for administrative positions at two-year institutions, Latinos have not advanced into administrative positions in California community colleges, despite affirmative action programs, legislation, and litigation (Rivera, 1985). Between 1973 and 1983, the majority of community colleges in California failed to recruit a single Latino candidate for an administrative opening (Rivera, 1985); thus the concentration of Latino faculty at two-year institutions has not increased their presence in the administrative ranks of two-year institutions (Acevedo, 1979; de los Santos, 1976).

Institutional Stratification of Latino Faculty

Several studies have examined Latino faculty's perceptions of academe, finding, not surprisingly, that the environment is isolating, alienating, and exploitative. For example, a study of the impact and use of Latino faculty within predominately white universities found that Latino faculty were used to incorporate minor changes in the curriculum, but not to play a significant role in making decisions about academic policy (Romero, 1977). Latino faculty could propose course offerings in Latino studies, but could not use such course offerings to structure an academic major or program in Latino studies.

Intergroup Perceptions

A study of the life experiences that shaped the educational careers of Latino students and faculty asked Latino faculty to identify problems they had as non-Anglo professionals (Astin & Burciaga, 1981). The Latino faculty in the study identified the following problems: (1) lack of institutional commitment to educational equality, especially in the recruitment of minority students and faculty; (2) difficulty in gaining acceptance and respect from their Anglo colleagues; and (3) lack of other minorities at their institution, which put an extra load on them (that is, the Latino faculty felt that they were expected to be institutional watchdogs). "Thus, Latino faculty, like other faculty of color, were more likely than were white faculty to view colleges and universities as racist and were much more committed to goals of educational equity" (Astin & Burciaga, 1981, p. 104).

Opportunity Structure

A set of descriptive data regarding the institutional participation of Latino faculty in academe was used to construct a set of observations regarding the social context surrounding Latino faculty in academe (Aguirre, 1987). According to these observations, the opportunity structure within academe constrains the participation of Latino faculty to minority-oriented activities. Further, Latino faculty are unable to decrease their participation in university service activities as they move up the academic ladder. Aguirre (1987) notes: "The observations constructed from the results presented suggest the presence of an organizational logic that sorts and channels Latino faculty into a limited opportunity structure in academe. The limitations imposed by this opportunity structure locate Latino faculty in activities that may be quite visible, yet are peripheral to the mainstream activity in the postsecondary organization" (p. 78).

Similarly, a study of Latino faculty attitudes toward the workplace notes that Latino faculty consider themselves excluded from decision making in their academic department, believe that the postsecondary institution uses them as buffers with the minority community, and perceive their campus as not supporting initiatives to improve the campus environment for minority students and faculty (Aguirre, 1987).

Perceptions of the Academic Environment

An examination of Latino perceptions about publication and research in academe found that while they subscribe to similar scholarly or academic values as white faculty, they believe that the university community and research/publication review committees do not accept them as equals or as scholars in their own right (Garza, 1989). Further, Latino faculty believe that their academic research about their own ethnic group is not rated as highly as research conducted by white faculty on Latinos. Similarly, a study of minority law professors notes that white peers often dismiss Latino faculty from consideration as serious scholars. For example: "A Latino applied to the LL.M. program at an eminent school to prepare for a teaching career. Although he had graduated from a top law school and first-rate undergraduate university and today is a tenured professor at a top-15 school, the chair of the LL.M. committee told him he would not be admitted because the school reserves its slots for persons of real intellectual caliber" (Delgado, 1988, p. 19).

The institutional relationship between Latino faculty and university administrators in academe places them in a situation of relative isolation, referred to as *barrioization.* "Colleges and universities have created a dumping ground for Latino scholars, separate from and with little interconnecting to the rest of the scholarly life of the university" (Garza, 1988, p. 124). In addition, the institutional isolation of Latino faculty is enhanced by an opportunity structure that shifts their institutional participation to peripheral activities (Aguirre, 1987).

Two factors contribute to the relative isolation of Latino and other faculty of color in academe: (1) overloading Latino faculty with minority-oriented institutional demands, such as service on university minority affairs committees, and (2) the lack of an established institutional network for faculty of color that could sponsor them within a variety of institutional sectors apart from minority-oriented activities (Escobedo, 1980). Latino faculty feel constrained by institutional demands that prevent them from participating in institutional sectors that are closer to mainstream decision making (Garza, 1989; Lopez & Schultz, 1980).

In a sense, then, the relative isolation of Latino faculty in academe has made them victims of "academic colonialism" because "whether one refers to Latino institutions, or Latino programs, or Latino personnel or students, the norm is for the organization loci of them to be in the periphery, in terms of participation in governance, academic credibility, recognition and status, resource allocation, permanence, and facilities" (Arce, 1978, p. 86).

As peripheral participants in academe, Latino faculty are unable to develop networks that could alter the perceptions white faculty hold of them. This contributes to the Latino faculty's neglect within academe. By ignoring Latino faculty, white faculty maintains Latino faculty's peripheral status. This is an institutional form of discrimination that impedes the progress of Latino faculty in academe (Luz Reyes & Halcon, 1991). In turn, the institutional discrimination preserves academe as a domain for white males (Bell, 1986; Bunzel, 1990; Valverde, 1975). It is also possible that recent gains made by white women in academe due to affirmative action have been at the expense of faculty of color (Cortese, 1992), so academe could now be the domain of both white males and white females.

Latino faculty share experiences similar to other faculty of color and women faculty in their interactions with the postsecondary institution (Aguirre, Martinez, & Hernandez, 1993). In particular, they all feel excluded from mainstream decision making and are overloaded with activities that target their status, such as race, ethnicity, and gender (Hu-Dehart, 1983; Lopez, 1991; Nieves-Squires, 1991). As a result, Latino faculty, like other faculty of color and white women faculty, occupy an organizational niche that enhances their powerless position in academe. This powerlessness becomes more acute if one assumes that exclusion from mainstream academic activities limits the social power and influence one can exert in academe.

In summary, the contextual feature of the postsecondary education institution's environment that best characterizes the status of Latino and other faculty of color is *exclusion*. The number of faculty of color in academe is too small for them to demand institutional changes, but is large enough for the institution to use them to further its own ends. The contextual character of Latino faculty in academe is best summed up as follows.

> As a Latino law professor, I fully appreciate the extent to which I and Latino colleagues have greater responsibilities; our service contributions and informal duties at times seem overwhelming. However, unless higher education takes more seriously its responsibilities to seek out others like us, and to behave differently toward Latinos, the extraordinary cycle of exclusion from faculty ranks will continue. Higher education is poorer for its loss. (Olivas, 1988, p. 9)

Thus, the nature of the exclusion of faculty of color is not limited to their invisibility within faculty ranks; it also affects their ability to identify with the environment of the institution of higher learning. The exclusionary practices are founded on a perspective of academe that suggests the circumstances serving as the basis for creating dilemmas in participation of faculty of color as marginalized faculty members.

A Perspective of Academe

The eighties were a time of economic growth but also of excessive selfishness; a time ideological walls crumbled as conceptual (and equally ideological) walls were erected; a time when the language of diversity was reintroduced but intolerance and provincialism also took their place at that same table.

The demographic facts of the nineties provide an insight into the lack of headway we have made to improve the circumstances of our diverse population. For example, one out of every four persons living today in the United States is of color, and one out of three will be a person of color in the year 2000. These demographic facts are having an inevitable impact on our educational system, from kindergarten to graduate school. They also place in a more formidable context the racial and ethnic insensitivity, discrimination, outright racism, and other institutional and personal acts of inequality that have been considered normal in academia.

Although our American political system has made a noble attempt at ensuring freedom and democracy for all people, these efforts have been greatly undermined by acts of figurative or actual exclusion perpetrated by institutions and individuals who consciously or unconsciously fear the loss of white privilege. McIntosh (1989) contends that "white privilege is like an invisible weightless knapsack of special provisions, maps, passports, code books, visas, clothes, tolls and blank checks" (p. 10). Thus, white privilege is an unusual container where social reality is constructed to perpetuate the dominance structures that are deemed normal.

Clearly, this hegemony is not free floating. It is bounded by and to the social reality of the state. As Apple (1985) indicates, hegemony is not an accomplished social fact but "a process in which dominant groups and classes manage to win the active consensus over whom they rule" (p. 29). The institutions within a society can be, and frequently are, sites of racial, gender, and class conflicts where "it must either force everyone to think alike or generate consent among a large portion of those contending groups" (p. 29).

Those with status and power sustain legitimacy power by continuously integrating many of the interests of allies and opponents. The process involves conflict, compromise, and an active struggle to maintain hegemony. Institutions of higher education foster and maintain the hegemony in which faculty of color function on a daily basis. Most of these faculty come from Vietnam War–era origins, were schooled in the sixties, and embarked on their professional careers in the seventies. These events are located within a contemporary history that has shaped situations for faculty of color. Theirs is a story of civil rights struggles, assassinations of national leaders, affirmative action, boycotts, national crises of political ethics, the mainstreaming of ethnic goods and services, multiculturalism, poverty in an affluent society, rapidly changing demographics, and political correctness.

As Padilla and Chavez Chavez (1995) note: "The temporal structure of everyday life in the everyday world imposes predefined social structures on the 'agendas' of any single day.—Indeed the clock and the calendar compel our Latina and Latino authors to be women and men of their time. For it is within a temporal structure that everyday life retains its accent of reality" (p. 3).

Even though faculty of color may have been disoriented by covert and overt prejudices, marginalized, and made to question their own humanity in the everyday experiences of academic life, these individuals have reoriented themselves. They reassert and reclaim their authenticity through leadership from the margin—that is, leadership through their words and actions and through their narratives as they voice their understanding of social reality. Through their leadership, they try to reconfigure their reality.

The voices of faculty of color are connected by at least two related premises. One condition encompasses the personal struggles with the various forms of *racism* that bound their institution. The second circumstance, *marginality,* is rooted in challenging prevailing paradigms in academic disciplines that display a provincialism that is neither reflective nor responsive to the experiences of communities of color.

Racism

Racism can be defined as a system of privileges and penalties based on one's race. It consists of two facets: (1) a belief in the inherent superiority of some people and the inherent inferiority of others; and (2) the acceptance of how goods and services are distributed in accordance with these judgments. Jones (1981) places racism into three categories: individual, institutional, and cultural. Individual racism is closest to racial prejudice and suggests a belief in the superiority of one's own race over another, while behaviorally it enacts an invidious distinction between races. Institutional racism is an extension of individual racism but includes manipulation of institutions so that one group benefits and maintains an advantage over others. Institutional racism supports practices that operate to restrict the choices, rights, mobility, and access of groups or individuals on a racial basis. Although not necessarily sanctioned by law, these practices are nevertheless real. Cultural racism includes the individual and institutional expression of the superiority of one race's cultural heritage over that of another race. Faculty of color encounter or witness all three categories of racism in varying degrees. Institutional racism is experienced as ideological and organizational pressures that reinforce and maintain social order to restrict entry into academia. Thus, in spite of possessing a doctoral degree, one is consistently denied opportunities in higher education.

Covert institutional practices of racism are well illustrated by the processes encountered in applications for promotion. In one case, Padilla (1995, p. 136) was facing a departmental review. Two of the individuals judging his work were associate professors. One of them had only one year in rank; the other lacked experience with doctoral students. The full professor on the committee was not familiar with Latino education, Padilla's area of expertise. Moreover, favorable judgments by knowledgeable full professors outside his department were accorded secondary importance. Reading between the lines, one can detect the department chair's protection and perpetuation of the status quo in the face of a review process that was clearly flawed.

Within the various networks in which most of us are engaged, we have heard many stories of the bigotry and intolerance faculty of color have experienced and of the privilege and power that is usually concentrated in the old guard (and, increasingly, the new wave of special interest groups). We see how racist superiority unfolds and how individual, institutional, and cultural racism are threaded into everyday life. For example, Mindiola's department chair told him that tenure and promotion standards had changed during his employment and that therefore he now needed more publications (Padilla & Chavez Chavez, 1995, pp. 29–52). Mindiola knew that the wife of one of the tenured professors in the department was also "going up" for tenure in the same department at this time. In addition, the tenured professor and his nontenured wife were part of the "influential political group in the department." The department chair, under the guise of being a supporter, gave advice to Mindiola, and after the third meeting, told Mindiola that he would probably be denied tenure. Mindiola believes that in this case the opposition to his bid for tenure was not motivated so much by prejudice but more by the department's need to tenure one of its own. Yet, university documents revealed that other non-Latino faculty with equal or lower accomplishments had been promoted and tenured.

Cruz (1995, pp. 91–100) challenges the subtle and not-so-subtle manifestations of institutional racism. Cruz was assigned to teach composition to foreign students. She learned the assignment was based on her own foreignness, although she was raised and socialized in the United States. People were stunned when Cruz revealed her research interest in nineteenth-century British literature. They asked why she wasn't interested in the literature of "her people." Later, when her own intellectual preoccupations led her to focus on ethnic literature, she faced the brown-on-brown research taboo (Luz Reyes & Halcon, 1988).

Racial incidents in higher education, similar to the ones described, were not well documented until the late sixties and early seventies when civil rights legislation compelled most universities to employ members from ethnically distinct groups. Once employed, such individuals and groups challenged prevailing personnel practices in higher education, particularly with respect to employee retention, tenure, and promotion. When individuals reported discrimination, bias, or underrepresentation of ethnically distinct groups, university authorities too often regarded them as isolated incidents even though they resulted in stereotyping, condescension transmitted as compliment, and the undermining of the academic work of faculty of color (Aronowitz, 1981). To characterize them as isolated only serves to perpetuate the status quo and stifles the debate that is needed to overcome them.

Marginality

The cultural milieu of institutions of higher learning experienced by Latino faculty (see Padilla & Chavez Chavez, 1995) suggests a narrow representative practice where Latinos and other faculty of color live on the fringe of the institution's community. Therefore, faculty of color have created concepts (for example, Ethnic Studies, Chicano Studies, Bilingual Education) that will promote a more popular practice. To do so, they have had to step out from the periphery of the institution onto the unknown and face the complexity of their community as well as the covert and overt racist acts carried out by entrenched forces in academia. As Rosaldo (1989, p. 92) reminds us, "we often improvise, learn by doing, and make up things as we go along." We are forced to live with ambiguity, uncertainty, and lack of knowledge every day. Then the day arrives when life's experiences clarify matters.

Even though marginality has many aspects that are difficult to pin down, it is a central theme for many faculty of color. They are marginalized but somehow integrated into their respective institutions. Although not necessarily marginalized in an economic or political sense, they are exploited in various ways and their creativity is often repressed. And while not necessarily marginalized socially and culturally, they are nevertheless stigmatized and excluded from many of the social networks in academia

(Perlman, 1975). Anzaldua (1990) describes marginality within the context of "womaness" and of "color," and notes that:

> The world knows us by our faces, the most naked, most vulnerable, exposed and significant topography of the body. When our caras do not live up to the "image" that the family or community wants to wear and when we rebel against the engraving of our bodies, we experience ostracism, alienation, isolation and shame. Since white Anglo-Americans' racist ideology cannot take in our faces, it, too covers them up, "blanks" them out of its reality." . . . Some of us are forced to acquire the ability, like a chameleon , to change color when the dangers are many and the options few. Some of us who already "wear many changes/inside of our skin" have been forced to adopt a face that would pass. (p. x)

Marginality becomes a constant balancing act that undermines the humanity and ethnic integrity of many of the faculty of color. Cruz (Padilla & Chavez Chavez, 1995, pp. 91–92), for example, wrestles with a confining institutional dominance and conquers it by accepting her cultural complexity. She tells how she was "designated as the spokesperson for all Latinos and Blacks." Cruz remembers the patronizing treatment of a faculty member who thanked her for "giving voice to the oppressed" when in actuality the faculty member was "congratulating herself for being liberal enough to 'empower' as if power can or should be given!" Cruz speaks of her marginalization. "No matter what we do (get a Ph.D., become wealthy, move out of the neighborhood), we are still separated and boxed into categories like 'ethnic' and 'minority.'"

The marginality Aguirre (1995, pp. 17–28) experiences comes as the feigned efforts to fulfill the mission of diversity in a multicultural world. He challenges pseudomulticultural academic values by giving us insight into what it is like to live as a stranger in academic paradise. To his students and to his academic colleagues, Aguirre is a stranger who, by his strangeness, is kept at the margin. He argues that minority faculty are placed in an "organizational niche from which (minorities) emerge only when academe needs them to legitimate its own response."

Aguirre, along with many of the other faculty of color believed in the myth that publishing was the brass ring to tenure, promotion, and academic success. Yet, faculty of color have been unable to maintain a steady, forceful academic presence within those networks that would help them advance their academic careers. Aguirre illustrates the hegemonic qualities of "reciprocal exclusivity" (Fannon, 1963) expected by those in power. That is, ethnically distinct men and women are compartmentalized into a climate that fosters "academic apartheid" by keeping such groups on the margins.

The marginalizing of a group can be very useful for those in power. Yet critical lessons are learned about the significance of bringing those who are marginalized into the mainstream via the practice of coalition politics. So the margins can become frontiers—cultural borders of the academic terrain where the Other takes a central role in configuring a counterhegemonic pedagogy. As Giroux (1992) reminds us:

> Indeed, such a task demands a rewriting of the meaning of pedagogy itself. It means comprehending pedagogy as a configuration of contextual, verbal, and visual practices that need to engage the processes through which people understand themselves and the ways in which they engage others and their environment. It recognizes that the symbolic presentations that take place in various spheres of cultural production in society manifest contest and unequal power relations. As a form of cultural production, pedagogy is implicated in the construction and organization of knowledge, desires, values, and social practices. At stake here is developing a notion of pedagogy capable of contesting dominant forms of symbolic production. (p. 3)

Dilemmas

Socialization into an academic community is problematic for people of color and white women because the professorate is overwhelmingly white male (Jensen, 1982). Reynolds (1992) argues that white women faculty and faculty of color experience more of an acculturation process than a socialization process since they must alter much of their individual identity.

Faculty and administrators of color represent diverse cultural backgrounds and face more of a *transformative socialization* (Luz Reyes & Halcon, 1991; Tierney, 1992). Based on a review of the literature, a number of dilemmas related to the socialization of faculty of color were identified: inadequate anticipatory socialization, weak mentoring relationships, fewer networking opportunities, diverse priorities, and additional work demands.

Inadequate Anticipatory Socialization

Some problems faculty of color face relate to *anticipatory socialization* (Turner & Thompson, 1993). Undergraduate and graduate schools introduce individuals to the prospective roles and expectations of various professions. Faculty of color and white women faculty report that as undergraduates they were encouraged less often than white males to pursue graduate work (Olsen, 1991). Blackwell (1984) notes that one-third of all doctoral students receive assistantships, but only one-fifth of minority doctoral students do.

A professor as a mentor is critically important in graduate school. Yet, underrepresented groups often have difficulty creating and sustaining such a relationship. Gender may compound dilemmas for faculty of color in developing helpful mentoring relationships (Aisenberg & Harrington 1988). For example, Rose (1985) reported that women tend to have weaker ties with their academic mentors. Clark and Corcoran (1986) noted a tendency for advisers and others to doubt a woman's potential for scholarly productivity.

Weak Mentoring of New Faculty of Color

Not only do faculty of color face difficulties in developing mentoring relationships during undergraduate and graduate school years, the same also may be said of their experiences as new faculty. Rausch, Ortiz, Douthitt, & Reed (1989) found that lack of institutional support for faculty was reported as a major factor in attrition. An ingredient in the support system is, of course, mentoring relationships. Here, again, lower percentages of faculty who left the institution reported receiving professional support from an informal mentor.

Few faculty of color benefit from a protégé-mentor relationship (Frierson, 1990). Only one in eight African American faculty identifies themselves with a mentor (Blackwell, 1983, 1984). Washington and Harvey (1989, p. 26) say that the lack of effective sponsorship was a significant problem for African American and Latino faculty. "The usual protective network of sympathetic senior faculty often does not exist."

Limited Networking Opportunities

Rose (1985) reported that women consistently rated their networks as less effective in helping them to build a professional reputation. Rose also noted that women had fewer ties to their previous institutions and had more women colleagues. One study reported that 47% of the African American faculty surveyed revealed feelings of isolation and alienation (Anderson, Frierson, & Lewis 1979). "They do not feel particularly close to white colleagues and often obtain little professional or emotional support" (p. 100). The lack of professional support networks is, in part, a by product of faculty of color being located at the periphery of teaching and research. "They are often in non-tenured positions or special programs for minorities" (Epps, 1989, p. 25).

Divergent Priorities

Some researchers have asked whether white women and faculty of color are socialized to recognize what activities are most important for academic success (Widom & Burke, 1978). Boice (1993) found that women value teaching to a greater degree than men. In a study of university faculty, Olsen (1991) discovered that faculty of color are more involved in service, white women are more involved in teaching, and white men are more involved in research. Of course, one needs to remember that research tends to be highly rewarded; consequently, such work habits partially explain the differential rates of tenure and promotion as well as higher attrition for white women and people of color.

Additional Demands

For faculty of color, additional demands relate to serving on campus committees where they frequently are selected to increase representation (Banks, 1984; Blackwell, 1988; Gilbert, 1990). Aguirre (1987) surveyed 149 Latino faculty in the southwest, reporting that 43% were involved in affirmative action or Mexican American community-related committees and 57% were on committees related to the recruitment and retention of Latino students. Cross (1991) highlighted some of the problems Native American faculty experience because of expectations placed on them to serve as counselors and advocates for Indian students as well as representing the Native American perspective on various campus committees.

Faculty of color face difficult decisions. They must decide to be either strict academics and advocate scholarship, or strict advocates and advocate community interests. On the one hand, their decisions are shaped by an academic culture that expects objective detachment. On the other hand, their communities need individuals who seek social action and political change (Garza, 1987).

Leadership from the Margin

From the university's point of view, the best vehicle for enhancing a faculty member's role in the academy is tenure and promotion. Yet, from the perspective of a faculty member of color, institutional expectations built into the dual identity of faculty of color hamper them in securing tenure and promotion. The trouble is not because of lack of productivity or competence but because of criteria application. The conventional criteria applied during tenure review are interpreted by white faculty members in such a way as to not accept faculty of color activities (mainly service to university and the field) as fulfilling the criteria (Valverde, 1981, p. 52).

Without a significant number of faculty of color in tenured and senior faculty positions, faculty of color will not be able to enter an institutional network that enhances their role as political brokers in academe. For example, because participation in some of the most powerful faculty senate committees is often limited to tenured senior faculty, the inability of Latinos to move into those ranks prevents them from participating in institutional activities that allocate resources, such as research grants. As participants in those activities, faculty of color could use the allocation of resources to sponsor untenured faculty of color in academe. That is, tenured faculty of color could facilitate the untenured faculty of color member's access to research grants. In turn, research support not only permits an untenured faculty member to pursue a research program, it also enhances his or her chances for tenure and promotion.

Can faculty of color become viable authoritative agents of leadership in a superficial multicultural academe? Probably not. In general, for faculty of color to become viable authoritative agents of leadership in a genuine multicultural academe, the opportunity structure that allocates privilege and power must be restructured. The chances that this change will occur are almost zero (Bunzel, 1990; Trow, 1992). Other correlates of faculty of color's presence in academe suggest their viability as agents of leadership.

First, excluding faculty of color from certain academic sectors and activities has resulted in a sense of "institutional marginality" among faculty of color. This, in turn, has facilitated postsecondary education's system of institutional discrimination regarding the participation of faculty of color in an institutional network that is necessary to build powerful alliances.

Second, the cognitive impact of institutional marginality is that faculty of color might perceive themselves as tokens in academe (Phillips & Blumberg, 1983). Although all faculty hold similar scholarly values, faculty of color feel that white faculty do not regard them as legitimate participants in academe (Garza, 1991). Rather, they think that faculty of color are participants as a result of institutional needs to meet external demands (such as affirmative action). If both faculty see faculty of color as tokens, then faculty of color will hesitate to participate in institutional activities or sectors that bestow political legitimacy. The issue is compounded for faculty of color because white faculty are the primary gatekeepers for those institutional sectors or activities.

This discourse is an effort to provide a practical framework from which to launch more focused debate about academic leadership for a truly multicultural academe. In this discussion, leadership means engaging people to make progress on problems encountered when there is no proven method, solution, clear-cut answer, or technical fix. Making progress on adaptive problems requires organizational learning (Senge, 1990). The task of leadership consists of orchestrating and directing learning processes within institutional boundaries (or in a community). Making progress often demands new ideas and innovation. It often requires changes in people's attitudes and behaviors. In this sense, change as "adaptive work" (Heifetz, 1994) is the process of discovering and making changes. Consequently, leadership from the margin in a multicultural academe requires an overt strategy (Burns, 1978, pp. 228–240).

This view of leadership provides a framework for assessing resources and developing leadership strategies premised on the assumption one has little or no formal power or status. Viewed in this way, for example, our questions about academic leadership and institutional development become: How can people with little or no formal status or power exercise leadership on issues without waiting for the institutional authorities with formal status and power?

Leading Without Status and Power

It is often asserted that leadership is too rarely exercised from high office (for example, that of a university administrator), and the constraints that come with formal authority go far to explain why (Bacow, O'Hare, & Sanderson, 1983). Faculty generally look to university administrators to solve problems with a minimum of pain (cost), and where pain can be endured, they often expect administrators to find somebody else to bear the costs. Many faculty, like members of any other formal organization, want change, as long as it occurs in someone else's social space. They too often expect university administrators to change the thinking and behavior of other people (for example, faculty of color and white women), rarely their own.

Thus, the scarcity of leadership from university administrators makes it even more critical that leadership be exercised by faculty, especially faculty of color who feel that they have little or no power or status in the institution. These individuals, frequently perceived as activists, organizers, entrepreneurs, or trouble makers, provide the capacity within an organization to see through the blind spots of a hegemonic point of view (Tucker, 1981). Often such persons are invisible, remaining relatively unknown, frequently beginning with no power or status but eventually gaining a broad base of influence. These are the voices who often push institutional members to clarify their values, face new realities, seize new possibilities in spite of held fears.

The literature on leadership without power and status is sparse (Heifetz, 1994). This paucity suggests neglect of distinctive problems and opportunities of mobilizing resources and organizational learning (Argyris, 1993). Much of the scholarship on leadership focuses on distinguished authority figures and is guided by the assumption that we are studying leaders and, thereby, understanding leadership. Heifetz (1994) suggests that the literature rarely reveals that leadership may often emerge from the "faces in the crowd," a place we rarely frequent.

It may be no accident that scholarly attention has neglected the mobilizing of leadership from positions of little or no power and status. A review of the literature reveals that studies of formal leadership frequently use metaphors that manifest images of white male dominance of leadership with authority. In contrast, leadership without authority has been projected as the domain of white women and people of color.

Having been denied formal authority roles in many societies, women have learned strategies for leading without formal power or status. The same can be said of disenfranchised groups of color, many of whom have learned not to try to lead at all. People of color who have managed to carve out roles of authority were usually ignored by traditional scholarship. Much of the contemporary attention to people of color and white women's leadership has occurred with the emergence of ethnic studies and women's studies as new academic fields where their accomplishments have been chronicled. With the study of leadership from the margin of institutions, perhaps our awareness of people of color and white women's leadership will increase as we simultaneously learn to authorize people of color and white women to positions from which they can lead institutions with formal authority.

Meanwhile, it is likely that individuals routinely go beyond their job description and informal expectations (as faculty of color often do) and do what they are not authorized to do. They exercise leadership by impressing on a group the need to pay attention to alternative, often invisible, points of view. For example, a faculty member will speak up at an administrative meeting even though she or he has no authority to do so. Often, in the early stage of a crisis (for example, a campus incident), some individuals will step forward and mobilize others to face and respond to the crisis. More publicly, faculty may publish a controversial perspective in, for example, a nonmainstream academic journal, book, or conference paper. Thus, when we speak of leadership from the margin, we are referring to a set of stances taken by a person with little or no status or power, operating from the periphery of an institution (university) and/or community.

Over time, an individual (or group) who begins without status or power may have to construct, strengthen and, occasionally, broaden her or his base of influence (for example, Black Studies, Chicano Studies) to get more leverage. As a result, she or he may find that an initial, rebellious leadership action puts her or him in a position of leadership that requires trust, respect, and moral force in order to sustain progress. Leadership from the periphery may require a base (for example, ethnic community or professional associations) from which to speak to hard issues without being ignored or rejected altogether. Moreover, to involve the relevant factions in the community, one may need people across boundaries to believe that he or she represents something significant, that he or she embodies a perspective that merits attention. If this happens, the individual exercising leadership from the margin of the institution has to respect the resources and constraints that come with legitimacy provided by a germane group and from beyond.

It is also important for one exercising leadership with little or no status or power to take counsel from his or her foes (the establishment), incorporating whatever wisdom gleaned from them is applicable to his or her concerns. As faculty of color seek informal authority from those across institutional or fractional boundaries, they must place their cause in the context of the values of competing colleagues (for example, diversity, academic excellence). It follows, then, that they may have to learn from their rivals in order to correct for the possible narrowness of their own views. In this case, they are not just guiding, they are also being guided. Consequently, faculty of color place and come to understand their struggle in the context of the prevailing hegemonic values and issues.

Heifetz (1995) suggests that faculty of color who lead without status or power may occasionally have to locate their contributions within an ongoing tradition or institution that provides a reservoir of assurance to hold the distress they generate. Since they have less leverage to shape the "holding environment,"[2] they must make use of the alliance that is there—for example, a colleague of the same ethnic background and/or gender status who listens with empathy to a distressful experience or who can tell a humorous story that not only fits the circumstances but will provide both a respite and a perspective that shields distress. That relationship is a holding environment.

Benefits of Leading from the Margin

Leadership with formal power and status (for example, a department chair, dean, vice president, president) generally includes power to: (1) manage relationships, social structures, and visions of the future; (2) direct attention; (3) gather and influence the flow of information; (4) frame the terms of debate; (5) distribute responsibility; (6) regulate conflict and distress; and (7) structure decision processes. Yet, these dimensions of authority imply that there may also be advantages to leading without authority. For example, leading without formal power and status:

- enables one to deviate from the norms of authoritative decision making. Instead of providing answers that soothe, one can readily raise questions that disturb. One does not have to keep the ship on an even keel;

- permits focusing hard on a single issue. One does not have to contend so fully with meeting the multiple expectations of multiple constituencies and providing the holding environment for everybody; and,

- places one closer to the detailed experiences of some of the stakeholders in the situation. One may lose the larger perspective but gain the finer grains of people's hopes, pains, values, habits, and history.

Strategies for Leading from the Margin

Because the benefits and constraints differ, those who lead without formal power and status must adopt strategies and tactics that are at once more daring and subtle. Heifetz (1994, p. 207) suggests several tactics, including: regulating the stimulus, monitoring institutional barometers, acting as a lightning rod, and mobilizing stakeholders.

Regulating the Stimulus

Without formal power, one has very little control over the parties involved in the decision-making process. One can shape the impetus, but can not manage the response, institute an organizing structure, pick a temporizing side issue, secure a new norm, or provide a calming presence. One with little or no power or status can spark debate, but cannot orchestrate it. Thus, one must regulate distress by regulating the stimulus. One may have a front-line feel for a single issue in depth, but not as broad a sense of the multiplicity of challenges facing the institution or community that affect its stance on any particular issue. This may render the person with little power or status less aware of the crucial problems confronting the institution or community and how fully developed their issue is in relation to other issues that may need to take priority.

For example, a faculty member of color, who was interested in the issue of access to higher education for nontraditional students of color, found the issue to be of little saliency to merit institutional attention. However, the faculty member quietly pursued his interest by developing a project that focused on recruitment and tutorial support to help minority students from a local urban school district achieve success in college. Over several years, the project gained a reputation as a model outreach program. Then the institution began to appreciate the symbolic value of the initiative and the constituency that the faculty built around it. It then acknowledged the issue by soliciting the faculty member's expertise to plan outreach initiatives. Thus, through his action, the faculty member generated energy, attention, questions, and some commitment to address the issue. Yet, as a result of becoming so involved in the initiative, he was captured by it. His perspective and actions were shaped by it to the degree that he became unaware of where the issue fit in the overall constellation of challenges facing the university. Consequently, his narrow focus on the issue shaped his stance on a number of other institutional issues, many of which were more significant.

Monitoring Institutional Barometers

In monitoring levels of distress, an individual has to find indicators for knowing both when to promote a less-developed issue and whether the stress generated by an intervention falls within the productive range for a particular institution at a particular time. Different institutional and community contexts will have different sources and levels of resilience, and each organization requires serious analysis. As a general rule, the individual operating with little or no power or status can read the authority figures as barometers of issue maturity and systemic stress because organizations generally charge administrators with the particular job of resolving full-fledged issues. Because a person exercising leadership without formal power is inclined to focus on a single issue, he or she will often have little information about the other sources of stress in the organization. He or she may challenge the institution too far and too fast and, thereby, invite his or her own suppression. Leadership from the margin, therefore, has to take into account the response patterns of the organization into which they intervene. Frequently, a person gains this understanding through trial and error, analyzing the sources of organizational wounds as they are acquired.

One barometer of organizational distress is the behavior of university administrators. Connected into the many issues facing the organization, university administrators tend to respond as a sum of the forces interacting. They are called into action as the stressed constituencies within their organization look upward for resolution, direction, protection, and order. Frequently, administrators respond to these appeals by acting to restore equilibrium, and their reaction reveals when the institution has reached the limits of its tolerance.

Of course, different university administrators will act differently. Each has their own distinct style: Some will encourage constituents to confront change, whereas others will cling to old realities. Whatever the reasons for the organizational distress, the administrators will, at some point, act to reduce the stress that they are perceiving. Typically, as a survival tactic, administrators are sensitive to the fears and expectations of those who authorize them. They are to some degree reactive to organizational stimuli, and, therefore, provide useful cues to those exercising leadership from the margin.

Acting as a Lightning Rod

In attracting and directing attention to an issue, an individual with little or no status or power has to take into account the special vulnerability of becoming a "lightning rod." Rather than orchestrating the debate among competing factions, one becomes a faction readily targeted for attack. Resources that are at the disposal of administrators for deflecting attention and for letting others take the lead are often unavailable to individuals leading from the margin.

As a result, gaining attention may not necessarily best serve one who is leading from the margin. These individuals often appear to be not only the identifier of a distressing problem but also the source of distress itself. All eyes turn to the individual who raises disturbing questions, and some, if not many, of those eyes are hostile. Campus constituencies may avoid problems by "shooting the messenger." Thus, although attention is a tool of leadership, it also makes one vulnerable to "targeting for attack." Leadership from the margin becomes vulnerable to people taking issue not only with the substance of an argument but also with the right of one to make the argument, frequently attacking the right instead of the substance.

The mechanisms for killing the messenger vary depending on the community, organization, and the problem. Yet, the attacks follow a general pattern:

- A person or faction raises a difficult question that generates some distress by pointing to a potential conflict over values and purpose, norms and organizational relationships, power, or strategy.

- For a response, disquieted members of the organization will focus their attention on organizational authority figures (administrators), seeking restoration of equilibrium.

- Authority figures, pressed by expectations to reduce distress, feeling compelled to respond, neutralize or silence the "problem" faction (Heifetz, 1994, p. 225).

A major challenge of leadership from the margin is to draw attention and then deflect it to the questions and issues that need to be faced. To do this, one has to provide a situation where the audience needs to readily comprehend the purpose of unusual behavior so that it focuses less on the behavior or the person and more on its meaning. Leadership from the margin must keep from becoming the issue by representing to the campus constituencies the issue for consideration.

For example, a Latino faculty member, who had recently been hired as full professor with tenure, was elected to replace a senior white male faculty as chair of a department. Being new to the institution and marginalized by the instructional role and service assignments given, the new chair became a lightening rod of attention on curricular reforms evolving in the college. His every move was subject to severe scrutiny, not only by the departmental faculty and staff but also by the authority structure of the college. Realizing that he was at the focal point, constantly at risk for making mistakes, the new chair used the lightening rod of attention to give life to an issue to which he wanted to draw attention—developing new faculty of color in academic leadership. All his actions revolved around the issue and had to be considered in that context. Thus, he never became the issue, as some desired, but simply represented the issue

Mobilizing Stakeholders

Just as institutional members look to those with formal power (administrators) to solve problems, those leading from the margin often make the mistake of assuming that only authority figures have the power to affect change. As a result, there is a tendency to identify the administrator as the audience for action. In general, however, people in power change their ways when the sources of their authority change expectations. Administrators' behavior is an expression of the stakeholders who authorize them. Thus, a strategy that mobilizes the stakeholders in the institution and community may more likely get work done than the strategy of challenging authority.

Those who lead from the margin have to give great attention to where they direct their leadership. The better their argument, the more they are likely to touch on an internal contradiction in the organization and thus arouse or aggravate conflicts, which then call forth administrative efforts to restore equilibrium. Hence, those who act without formal power in a way that generates distress for the organizational authority structure should expect administrators to react to campus constituencies' pressures to maintain equilibrium. It is important to underscore that rejection on the part of university administrators is more likely to be motivated by dominant institutional stakeholders who resist a disturbance of their equilibrium. The administrator is their proxy, serving their expectations.

In sum, any leadership exercised from the margins of the institution must focus on mobilizing the stakeholders, not their proxies. To do this one may need to address such questions as:

- Who are the primary stakeholders in the issue at hand?

- How may these stakeholders need to change their ways?

- What expectations do they have of the administrators?

- How can the administrators begin to reshape those expectations to provide themselves with latitude to take action?

- What can one do, exercising leadership without authority, to reshape those expectations?

Conclusion

In conclusion, the number of faculty of color is still rather small, and the population of Latino faculty has not grown appreciably in almost two decades. As a result, faculty of color are still relatively new entrants to academe. Further, institutions tend to exclude faculty of color from participation in it. By using an opportunity structure that focuses Latinos and other faculty of color on minority-oriented activities, postsecondary institutions marginalize these faculty away from mainstream activities. In turn, those marginalizing practices make these faculty peripheral participants in institutional leadership processes. In a sense, faculty of color are victims of "academic colonialism"; that is, they exist only as fabricated actors who meet the institutional needs and demands of academe for sustaining a particular equilibrium.

The nature of their participation in academe creates a number of dilemmas for faculty of color. As a result of the dilemmas and their treatment as peripheral participants, it is difficult for faculty of color to mature as potential sources of institutional leadership. Moreover, their relatively powerless position prevents them from establishing an institutional network that could lead to constructive academic alliances supportive of effective role-modeling activities and productive sponsoring of nontraditional students and faculty. The ascription of a dual identity for faculty of color enhances their invisibility by forcing them to participate in institutional activities or sectors white faculty do not regard as legitimate vehicles for tenure and promotion.

Academic custom and precedence play a major role in the recruitment and retention of faculty of color and white women faculty and their overall socialization experiences (Exum, 1984). Socialization that honors difference is about rethinking custom and precedence. It is not only about an institutional willingness to change, to be flexible, to become more inclusive of cultural diversity, it is also about expressing this willingness by restructuring power and status relationships to allow for changing leadership needs. To recruit faculty of color and white women faculty without creating structures that encourage the reshaping of the organizational culture is an assimilationist endeavor prone to failure, as evidenced by the attrition of faculty from diverse groups. As Simeone (1987) states: "It would not be sufficient for higher education simply to increase the numbers of women and minorities within the system if that system continues to be male-dominated in its policies, practices, epistemologies, values, methodologies, and structures" (p. 21).

If faculty of color are to become viable agents of leadership in an authentic multicultural academe, structural and institutional issues must be addressed. First, the hierarchical arrangement of privilege and power in academe must be restructured to provide faculty of color with access. Second, faculty of color presence must increase within the tenured ranks of the faculty. Third, white faculty must alter their perception that faculty of color are tokens and are present in academe only as a result of external demands on academe to sustain hegemony. While attaining these kinds of conditions does not guarantee how academe will respond to or treat faculty of color, it does serve as a vehicle for defining the equitable participation of faculty of color in leadership for a multicultural academe.

NOTES

1. The term "Latinos" refers to individuals whose ancestors originated in a Spanish-speaking country and who may identify themselves as Latinos, Mexican Americans, or other similar national origin labels.

2. The term "holding environment" originated in psychoanalysis to describe the relationship between the therapist and the patient. The therapist "holds" the patient in a process of developmental learning. Heifetz (1994) extends the use of the concept to a "holding environment of any relationship in which one party has power to hold the attention of another party and facilitate adaptive work" (pp. 104–105) (for example, coach and team, teacher and students, manager and staff).

REFERENCES

Acevedo, B. (1979). Socialization: Chicano administrators in higher education. *Emergent Leadership, 3,* 28–41.

Aguirre, A, Jr. (1987). An interpretative analysis of Chicano faculty in academe. *Social Science Journal, 24,* 71–81.

Aguirre, A, Jr. (1995). A Chicano farmworker in academe. In R. Padilla & R. V. Chavez Chavez (Eds*.), The leaning ivory tower: Latino professors in American universities* (pp. 17–28). Albany: State University of New York Press.

Aguirre, A., Jr., R. Martinez, & A. Hernandez. (1993). Majority and minority faculty perspectives in academe. *Research in Higher Education, 344,* 371–385.

Aisenberg, N., & Harrington, M. (1988). *Women of academe: Outsiders in the sacred grove.* Amherst: University of Massachusetts Press.

Anderson, W., Jr., H. Frierson, & T. Lewis. (1979). Black survival in white America. *Journal of Negro Education, 48,* 92–102.

Anzaldua, G. (1990). Haciendo caras a la entrada. In G. Anzaldua (Ed*.), Making face, making soul, haciendo caras: Creative and critical perspectives by women of color* (pp. xv–xxiii). San Francisco: Aunt Lute Foundation.

Apple, M. W. (1985). *Education and power.* Boston: Ark Paperbacks.

Arce, C. (1976). Chicanos in higher education. *Integrated Education, 14,* 14–18.

Arce, C. (1978). Chicano participation in academe: A case of academic colonialism. *Grito del Sol: A Chicano Quarterly, 3,* 75–104.

Argyris, C. (1993) *Knowledge for action: A guide to overcoming barriers to organizational change.* San Francisco: Jossey-Bass.

Aronowitz, S. (1981). *The crisis in historical materialism.* New York: Praeger.

Astin, H., & Burciaga, C. (1981). *Chicanos in higher education: Progress and attainment.* ED 226 690. 179 pp. MF-01; PC-08.

Bacow, L., O'Hare, M., & Sanderson, D. (1983). *Facility siting and public opposition.* New York: Van Nostrand Reinhold.

Banks, W. M. (1984). Afro-American scholars in the university. *American Behavioral Scientist, 27,* 325–338.

Bell, D. (1986). Strangers in academic paradise: Law teachers of color in still white schools. *University of San Francisco Law Review, 20,* 385–395.

Blackwell, J. E. (1983). *Networking and mentoring: A study of cross-generational experiences of black professionals.* Bayside, NY: General Hall.

Blackwell, J. E. (1984, October). *Increasing access and retention of minority students in graduate and professional schools.* Paper presented at the Educational Testing Services Invitational Conference on Educational Standards, Testing, and Access, New York.

Blackwell, J. E. (1988). Faculty issues: Impact on minorities. *The Review of Higher Education, 11,* 417–434.

Boice, R. (1993). New faculty involvement for women and minorities. *Research in Higher Education, 34,* 291–341.

Bunzel, J. (1990). Minority faculty hiring: Problems and prospects. *American Scholar, 59,* 39–52.

Burns, J. M. (1978). *Leadership.* New York: Harper Colophon.

California State University. (1984). *Hispanics and higher education: A CSU imperative.* Long Beach, CA: Office of the Chancellor.

Carter, D. J., & Wilson, R. (1992). *Minorities in higher education.* Washington, DC: American Council on Education.

Clark, S. M., & Corcoran, M. (1986). Perspectives on the professional socialization of women faculty. *Journal of Higher Education, 57,* 20–43.

Committee on Education and Labor. (1984). *Hearings on the Reauthorization of the Higher Education Act before the Subcommittee on Postsecondary Education.* Washington, DC: U.S. Government Printing Office. ED 254 144. 1,493 pp. MF-12; PC-60.

Cortese, A. (1992). Affirmative action: Are white women gaining at the expense of black men? *Equity and Excellence, 25,* 77–89.

Cross, W. T. (1991). Pathway to the professoriate: The American Indian faculty pipeline. *Journal of American Indian Education, 30,* 13–24.

Cruz, D. M. (1995). Struggling with labels that mark my ethnic identity. In R. Padilla & R. Chavez Chavez (Eds.), *The leaning ivory tower: Latino professors in American universities* (pp. 91–100). Albany: State University of New York Press.

de los Santos, A. (1976). Emerging Chicano administrators in higher education. *Emergent Leadership, 1,* 17–19.

Delgado, R. (1988). *Minority law professors' lives: The Bell-Delgado survey.* Working Papers Series 3. Madison: University of Wisconsin-Madison, Law School Institute for Legal Studies.

Epps, E. G. (1989). Academic culture and the minority professor. *Academe, 75,* 23–26.

Escobedo, T. (1980). Are Hispanic women in higher education the nonexistent minority? *Educational Researcher, 9,* 7–12.

Esquibel, A. (1977). *The Chicano administrator in colleges and universities of the southwest.* Doctoral dissertation, University of New Mexico, Albuquerque.

Exum, W. (1984). Making it to the top. *American Behavioral Scientist, 27,* 303–324.

Fanon, F. (1963). *The wretched of the earth.* New York: Grove Press.

Frierson, H. T., Jr. (1990). The situation of black educational researchers: Continuation of a crisis. *Educational Researcher, 19,* 12–17.

Garza, H. (1988). The "barrioization" of Hispanic faculty. *Educational Record, 68/69,* 122–124.

Garza, H. (1989). *Second-class academics: Chicano/Latino faculty in U.S. universities.* Unpublished manuscript. Fresno: California State University at Fresno, Department of Chicano and Latin American Studies.

Garza, H. (1991). *Academic power, discourse, and legitimacy: Minority scholars in U.S. universities.* Unpublished manuscript. Fresno: California State University at Fresno, Department of Chicano and Latin American Studies.

Gilbert, C. T. (1990, March). *Minority faculty recruitment & retention in higher education.* Paper presented at the U.S. Department of Education Special Hearing, Indian Nations at Risk Task Force, Phoenix.

Giroux, H. (1992). *Border crossings:Cultural workers and the politics of education.* New York: Routledge.

Heifetz, R. A. (1994). *Leadership without easy answers.* Cambridge: Harvard UniversityPress.

Hu-Dehart, E. (1983). Women, minorities, and academic freedom. In C. Kaplan & E. Schrecker (Eds.), *Regulating the intellectuals: Perspectives on academic freedom in the 1980's* (pp. 231–260). New York: Praeger.

Jensen, K. (1982). Women's work and academic culture: Adaptations and confrontations. *Higher Education, 11,* 67–83.

Jones, J. M. (1981). *The concept of racism and its changing reality.* In B. P. Bowser & R. G. Hunt (Eds.), *Impacts of racism on white Americans* (pp. 8–23). Beverly Hills, CA: Sage Publications.

Katsinas, S. (1984). Hispanic students and staffing patterns in community colleges. ED 248 904. 17 pp. MF-01; PC-01.

Lopez, A., & Schultz, R. (1980). Role conflict of Chicano administrators in community colleges. *Community College Review, 7,* 50–55.

Lopez, T. (1991). *Some African American and Hispanic voices from the University of Toledo (Ohio).* ED 328 15. 5 pp. MF-01; PC-03.

Luz Reyes, M. de la, & Halcon, J. J. (1988). Racism in academia: The old wolf revisited. *Harvard Educational Review, 58*(3), 299–314.

Luz Reyes, M. de la, & Halcon, J. J. (1991). Practices of the academy: Barriers to access for Chicano academics. In P. G. Altbach and K. Lomotey (Eds.), *The radical crisis in American higher education* (pp. 168–175). Albany: State University of New York Press.

McIntosh, P. (1989). White privilege: Unpacking the invisible knapsack. *Peace and Freedom,* July/August, 10–12.

Milem, J., & Astin, H. (1993). The changing composition of the faculty: What does it really mean for diversity? *Change, 25,* 21–27.

Nieves-Squires, S. (1991). *Hispanic women: Making their presence on campus less tenuous.* Washington, DC: Association of American Colleges, Project on the Status and Education of Women. ED 334 907. 16 pp. MF-01; PC-01.

Olivas, M. (1979). *The dilemma of access: Minorities in two-year colleges.* Washington, DC: Howard University Press.

Olivas, M. (1988). Latino faculty at the border, *Change, 2,* 6–8.

Olsen, D. (1991). Gender and racial differences among a research university faculty: Recommendations for promoting diversity, *To Improve the Academy, 10,* 123–139.

Padilla, R. V. (1995). Memorabilia from academic life. In R. V. Padilla & R. Chavez Chavez (Eds.), *The leaning ivory tower: Latino professors in American universities* (pp. 131–150). Albany: State University of New York Press.

Padilla, R. V., & Chavez Chavez, R. (Eds.). (1995). *The leaning ivory tower: Latino professors in American universities.* Albany: State University of New York Press.

Perlman, J. (1975). Rio's faveles and the myth of marginality. *Politics and Society, 5,* 121–160.

Phillips, W., & Blumberg, R. (1983). Tokenism and organizational change. *Integrated Education, 20,* 34–39.

Rausch, D. K., Ortiz, B. P., Douthitt, R. A., & Reed, L. L. (1989). The academic revolving door: Why do women get caught? *CUPA Journal, 40,* 1–15.

Reynolds, A. (1992). Charting the changes in junior faculty: Relationships among socialization, acculturation, and gender. *Journal of Higher Education, 63,* 637–652.

Rivera, M. (1985, May). *El cedazo: Sifting and shifting or the Hispanic participation in the management of the California community colleges, 1973–83.* Paper presented at an annual conference of the Texas association of Chicanos in Higher Education, McAllen. ED 274 469. 44 pp. MF-01; PC not available EDRS.

Romero, D. (1977, July). *The impact and use of minority faculty within a university.* Paper presented at an annual meeting of the American Psychological Association, San Francisco.

Rosaldo, R. (1989). *Culture and truth: The remaking of social analysis.* Boston: Beacon Press.

Rose, S. M. (1985). Professional networks of junior faculty in psychology. *Psychology of Women Quarterly, 9,* 533–547.

Senge, P. M. (1990). *Fifth discipline: The art and practice of organizational learning.* New York: Doubleday.

Simeone, A. (1987). *Academic women: Working towards equality.* South Hadley, MA: Bergin & Garvey.

Tierney, W. G. (1992). *Official encouragement, institutional discouragement: Minorities in academe: The Native American experience.* Norwood, NJ: Ablex.

Trow, M. (1992). Class, race, and higher education in America. *American Behavioral Scientist, 35,* 585–605.

Tucker, R. C. (1981). *Politics as leadership.* Columbia: University of Missouri Press.

Turner, C.S.V., & Thompson, J. R. (1993). Socializing women doctoral students: Minority and majority experiences. *The Review of Higher Education, 16,* 355–370.

Uribe, O., & Verdugo, R. (1990, March). *A research note on the status and working conditions of Hispanic faculty.* Paper presented at the annual meeting of the American Educational Research Association, Boston.

Valverde, L. (1975). Prohibitive trends in Chicano faculty employment. In H. Casso & G. Roman (Eds.), *Chicanos in higher education* (pp. 12–15). Albuquerque: University of New Mexico Press.

Valverde, L. (1981). Achieving equity in higher education: Inclusion and retention of Hispanic academics. In T. Escobedo (Ed.), *Education and Chicanos: Issues and research.* Monograph No. 8. Los Angeles: University of California at Los Angeles, Spanish-Speaking Mental Health Research Center.

Valverde, L. (1988). The missing element: Hispanics at the top in higher education. *Change, 20,* 11.

Valverde, L, & Ramirez, E. (1977). Chicano professionals in Texas higher education: A statistical summary. *El Cuaderno, 1,* 26–30.

Verdugo, R. R. (1992). Analysis of tenure among Hispanic higher education faculty. *AMAE Journal* (Special Edition: *Chicanos in Higher Education*), 23–30.

Verdugo, R. R. (1995). Racial stratification and the use of Hispanic faculty as role models: Theory, policy and practice. *Journal of Higher Education, 66,* 669–685.

Washington, V., & Harvey, W. (1989). *Affirmative rhetoric, negative action: African American and Hispanic faculty at predominantly white institutions.* ASHE ERIC Higher Education Report No. 2. Washington, DC: Association for the Study of Higher Education. ED 316 075. 128 pp. MF-01; PC-06.

Widom, C. S., & Burke, B. W. (1978). Performance, attitudes and professional socialization of women in academia. *Sex Roles, 4,* 549–562.

Five Recommendations to Build a Multicultural Campus

Faculty
Vanessa Allen-Brown

- The department should *introduce* African American women faculty to the local community to establish a more supportive environment for these new faculty.

- The department should *encourage* African American women faculty to network with other women faculty across units on campus.

- The department should *obtain* quality information on what cultural differences exist among female faculty and factor those issues into the unit's plan for diversity.

- The department must *affirm* African American women faculty's right to take *corrective* action (for example, meeting with chair or dean) whenever their value is marginalized in the reward system.

- The department must *accept* and *recognize* the tremendous and arguably unique service expectation the larger community has for African American female faculty.

Eight

African American Women Faculty and Administrators:

Surviving the Multiple Barriers of Discrimination

Since the 1970s, the literature (Collins, 1991; Williams, 1989) indicates that with the help of special interest groups and government regulations, there has been substantial progress for women entering higher education. Women's rights groups helped press for (as well as monitored) legislation prohibiting sex discrimination in educational institutions. Affirmative action gave women a legal claim to fair and equal treatment to employment opportunities, including salary, tenure, and promotion (Fleming, Gill, & Swinton, 1978; Washington & Harvey, 1989). Women caucuses and commissions of professional associations help promote women's scholarship and develop strategic roles for women's studies (Chamberlain, 1989).

Even with the progress since the 1970s, gender discrimination continues to hinder the achievement of women faculty and administrators in higher education. In all types of institutions, studies show that women are under-represented and progress more slowly through the ranks than white males.

Hensel (1991) contends that it will take women 90 years to achieve equal representation to the men on these campuses. Women are concentrated in the lower ranked and nonladdered untenured positions and in traditional women's fields. They are disproportionately involved in teaching and have longer hours and larger class sizes. Yet, women receive substantially less compensation and benefits compared to their male counterparts. Finally, women have very limited positions in male-dominated academic departments and professional schools. Because of their marginal positions, many women lack access to the decision-making process on their campuses (Theodore, 1986).

However, a closer examination of the data reveals that African American women are even further away than Euro American women in achieving equality within the academy. Described as victims of "double jeopardy" (Carter, Pearson, & Shavlik, 1988), Black women's access to faculty and administrative positions is impeded by both racial and gender discrimination. Studies show that before the 1970s, the majority of African American women were concentrated in the 114 historically Black colleges and universities (Swann & Witty, 1980). Current data reveal that the majority of Black women are still concentrated within these institutions (Elam, 1989).

Although the data may imply that Black women have made significant gains in higher education, their progress is certainly not equal to that of white males or white females. According to current research, Black women continue to be less likely than white men to go to college. In 1985, for example, white men received 37% of all associate's degrees (429,823), 42% of all bachelor's degrees (968,311), 38% of all master's degrees (280,421), 46% of all doctorates (32,307), and 60% of all first professional degrees (971,057). Minority males received 7% of all associate's degrees, 5% of all bachelor's degrees, 5% of all master's degrees, 6% of all first professional degrees, and 6% of all doctoral degrees.

White women, in the same year, received 46% of all associate's degrees 43% of all bachelor's degrees, 42% of all master's degrees, 28% of all doctorates, and 29% of all first-professional degrees. Black women, on the other hand, received more than one-half of the degrees awarded to minority women in 1985. In that year, they earned 5% of all associates degrees, 4% of all bachelor's degrees, 3% of all master's degrees, and 2% each of all doctorates and first-professional degrees (Touchton & Davis, 1991). Data further show that the educational gains made by Black women were heavily concentrated in the early 1970s (Astin, 1982). Chamberlain (1989) contended that during this time, the enrollment rates of Black women rose from 66% to 82% of those of white women and from 42 to 82% of those for white men (p. 40). Yet, by the end of the decade, graduate and undergraduate enrollment began to taper off.

Most disturbing is the decline in graduate enrollment, which is the pool from which faculty and administrators are ordinarily drawn. Some have argued that this leveling off is even more distressing because it occurred in an era when there was a good deal of financial aid, including state funds for doctorates, and federal mandates (Washington & Harvey, 1989). By the end of the eighties, less financial aid was available. Chamberlain (1989) suggests that the lack of financial assistance may have encouraged African American women to enter professional schools. As a result, Menges and Exum (1983) and Washington and Harvey (1989) argue that business and private industry may be claiming the best African American women students by offering them more money and better working conditions, once again limiting the pool from which Black faculty and administrators are drawn.

With these observations in mind, how does one view the current status of African American women faculty and administrators in the academic profession? To understand their level of involvement as well as their contribution to the academy, it is necessary to examine their proportionate presence, including distribution by institutional type, discipline, rank, and promotion.

The proportion of full-time faculty who are women increased slightly between 1975 and 1985, from 25% (95,674) to 28% (118,798). At the same time, the proportion of women faculty who are minorities remained steady at 12%. Although only 3% of all full-time faculty members were minority women, there was a 23% (12,535 15,415) increase in the number of minority women faculty in that ten-year period. At the same time, the number of Black women faculty increased by 4% from 8,852 to 9,230 (Touchton & Davis, 1991).

Black women continue to be primarily concentrated in the 114 predominantly Black institutions. On these traditional Black college campuses, Elam (1989) found that Black women constituted 24% of the full professors (482), 32% of the associate professors (827), 46% of the assistant professors (1,565), and 53% of the instructors (806). However, Black women are disproportionately located in less-prestigious four-year colleges and universities, and in public rather than private colleges. They are particularly underrepresented at major research institutions (Menges & Exum, 1983;

Finkelstein, 1984; Washington & Harvey, 1989). In these institutions, Black women faculty members have the lowest faculty progression, retention, and tenure rates. They are also concentrated in the lower academic ranks (Chamberlain, 1989; Graves, 1990; Wilson, 1987). In 1991, of the 52,479 tenured women faculty, 3,627 (7%) were Black. Black women constituted only 1.9% of full-time faculty in higher education; they made up 0.6% of full professors, 1.4% of associate professors, 2.7% of assistant professors, and 3% of instructors, lecturers, and others (cited in Elam, 1989).

In disciplinary fields, Finkelstein (1984) found that African American women were more likely to be found in education and the social sciences, especially in Black or ethnic studies departments. They were distributed evenly between the humanities and the natural sciences. Among doctoral scientists, Black women were found in mathematics and chemistry. In 1981, minority women's representation in the pool of doctoral scientists and engineers increased by 10.9%. Within this group, Chamberlain (1989) found that though the number of Black women scientists increased, they remained a constant percentage of the pool of minority scientists. Of the 7,340 minority women among the doctoral scientists and engineers in 1985 (1.72%), 0.42% were African American, an increase of .30%.

The data indicate that African American women are a small proportion of faculties in higher education. They are also a small proportion of the administrative structure. In 1985, 43,698 women (35% of a total of 124,374) were full-time executives, managers, or administrators in higher education institutions. Of these women administrators, 86% were white, non-Hispanic, and only 10% were Black (EEO-6 Summary Report). The data suggest that Black women are most likely to be found as director of Affirmative Action/ Equal Employment, and next most likely to be found as director of Financial Aid or director of Student Counseling (Chamberlain, 1989; Fulton, 1983; Graves, 1990; Tinsley, Secor, & Kaplan, 1984; Touchton & Davis, 1991). Wilson (1989) found that although women of color were better represented in administrative positions below the presidential level, they occupied, in minimal numbers, presidencies in all types of institutions. He found that Black women were better represented as presidents in predominantly white universities than as presidents of historically Black colleges. They were also found more in community colleges and public institutions.

The literature on Black women faculty and administrators reveals that they are not educated or hired according to their proportional presence within the society. Based on the literature, we can draw four conclusions about the current status of African American women faculty and administrators. First, they continue to lag in their proportional representation as faculty and administrators. Second, they are disproportionately represented in the lower ranks. Third, they play very minimal roles aš administrators. Fourth, they are primarily concentrated in education and several areas of the social sciences.

Area of Concern

As discussed above, African American women in academe are under-represented in major research institutions, are disproportionately located in less-prestigious four-year colleges and universities, and are found in public rather than private colleges. The data suggest several areas of study that are essential for understanding their achievements as faculty and administrators. However, research on African American women has primarily concentrated on their failure to achieve the same educational and career attainment as the majority population. Chamberlain (1989), for example, argued that although "whites have continued to increase their educational attainment, minorities for the most part continue to lag behind the majority population" (p. 37).

In reference to career attainment, the small percentage of African American women receiving doctorates appears to have a direct correlation to the small percentage of African American women faculty and administrators (Carter, Pearson, & Shavlik, 1988; Graves, 1990; Smith, 1985). So much so that Myrtis Mosley (1980) claimed Black women administrators are an endangered species. Yet, Washington and Harvey (1989) caution against the cure-all to "simply increase the number of Ph.D.s" in the availability pool (p. 52). They argue, along with others (Trueba, in this volume), that even when the number of Ph.D.s increased, search committee chairs often reported they couldn't find any qualified minority candidates. Most of the research on African American women in higher education typically focuses on the reasons why there are so few African American women faculty and administrators rather than examining factors that contribute to their achievement within the academy.

In contrast, the study discussed below examines internal and external factors that contributed to the achievement of African American women in higher education. It focuses on personal factors (personality traits), socialization and cultural influences (societal sex-role stereotypes), socioeconomic background factors (occupational and educational level), and institutional barriers (racial and gender discrimination).

Our Story

In soliciting my informants' stories, I discovered that our stories were intertwined. The selection of the interview questions, the coding, and analysis procedures all established a kindred relationship between us. Our stories provide insight into campus life for African American women in higher education. African American women share the same kinds of struggles for achievement and received supportive from their respective communities, family, and friends. My story and those of my informants are one.

Twenty African American women in higher education from across the United States participated in this study. I analyzed their narratives using the ground theory approach (Strauss & Corbin, 1990). I selected events and incidents from their narratives that illuminated my evolving theory of African American women's achievement in academe. In particular, I selected information about what they did or didn't do in terms of: their relationships within the academy, their homes, and communities; the influence of socialization and structural factors and their variations on them; how national trends and policies changed or stayed the same over time and with what impact; and the consequences of either actual or failed action/interaction or of strategies never acted on (Strauss & Corbin, 1990).

A semistructured interview format covered the major questions in the study and encouraged the women to tell their story with a minimum of interruption. Through constant comparative analysis, categories emerged from the data that provided an understanding of factors that contribute to the achievement of African American women faculty and administrators. These categories are (1) Racial Identity, (2) Gender Identity, (3) National Policies and Trends, (4) Support Networks, (5) Church, (6) Personal Beliefs, and (7) Escapism.

Racial Identity

In this category, participants discussed how race played a role in their development and decision making. This was evident in the teachings of parents and in the expectations of the African American community. Both influenced the participants' achievements by instilling within them pride about themselves and about their race. This category also reflected the struggles and pain that family members endured in their search for acceptance.

> I was encouraged by my heritage. It was ingrained in me. It was a reflection of my race and my family. It was drilled into me that my parents did not get things because of racism. I really believed that my heritage was significant. Because if someone told me I could not do something, I would ask was it me or my race. It made me push harder. In many instances, I felt like I was a pioneer. My heritage (or my ethnicity) is very much a driving force. (Esther Long, administrator)

The research of Allen and Majidhi-Ahi (1989) supports this teaching as a form of socialization. African American parents, they claim, are forced to encourage their children's development of achievement motivation, self-confidence, and self-esteem. These characteristics are seen as essential for their children's survival in a racist society. Although racial pride was taught, the women were also instructed to remember that they lived in two distinct worlds, one black and one white. To survive, it was imperative that they learned to function within both of these worlds, "not forgetting from where you come" (sic). Katie Cannon (1985) described the two worlds as contradictory: "one white, privileged, and oppressive, the other Black, exploited, and oppressed" (p. 30). Within these two worlds, she contended, Black women struggle for survival. One administrator shared her mother's strategy for surviving in these two distinct worlds.

Racial identity also influenced the participants' ambivalence toward assimilation into mainstream culture. They voiced a distrust of Euro American's tolerance for cultural and racial differences. Similar findings were supported by Blackwell (1991). He argued that because African Americans do not have equal access to the shared values within the opportunity structure, they are not assimilable into American society. When asked to what extent they had assimilated, the women used such phrases as "never," "not even slightly," "forget it," "very little," or "I do what I have to do to survive." When asked to elaborate, one participant stated:

> I'm sure from the surface you're looking at a Black woman, Ph.D. . . . I travel over 150,000 miles a year. I have a platinum American Express card. . . . But no, I'm not assimilated. I know their game, I know their rules, I know how to play it. I'm definitely bicultural. Yeah, I can switch it on and off. (Michele Banks, faculty)

The expectations of the Black community and the shared culture of segregated schools supported the women's racial identity and encouraged them to achieve. The women spoke of receiving words of praise and discipline from teachers, neighbors, and church members. The women interpreted these words as motivation for them to achieve. Participants who attended segregated schools (75% elementary and 40% high school) also described that as an experience that influenced their achievement positively. These schools functioned as extensions of the family and served the needs of the larger communities. In addition, the presence of African American teachers and students was a bond between those who shared the same ethnic heritage. These findings are supported by Blackwell (1991), Collins (1991), and McAdoo (1988), who agree that despite their racial isolation, African Americans developed communities that provided mutual support and social control. The participants understood that the individual was a reflection of the community. Therefore, her achievements were tied to those of the community:

> I went to segregated schools. So until I graduated from high school, I always had all Black teachers. I think it made a difference, because they were people from my ethnic group who were proud of me because I was a reflection of them. (Kimberly Brown, administrator)

Gender Identity

In this category, the participants' identity as females was significant in their development and decision making. Their perception of social reality and social interactions affected their choices and decisions to pursue higher education and develop nontraditional career goals. Mothers had the greatest influence on their daughters' understanding of their identity and the choices they made as a result. They were socialized to have a positive self-concept, to be instrumental, expressive, androgynous, and to have liberal attitudes toward women's roles. These personality and attitudinal characteristics are thought by some to be significant indicators for women's achievement (Betz & Fitzgerald, 1987; Farmer, 1985; Fassinger, 1985; Gilbert, 1985; Gilligan, 1990; Murray, 1981).

Participants were also socialized to value education and achievement. They internalized the belief that education was synonymous with independence and that it ranked above chores or attitudes that are usually associated with women's roles in society. Participants were taught that an education would lead to upward mobility. These findings are inconsistent with several studies about gender and education. Williams (1989) argued that women are socialized to work for love, approval, and affiliation rather than achievement. As a result, their self-esteem is tied to external rather than internal sources of personal affirmation. Sadker and Sadker (1994) report that conflict emerges for girls during and after puberty because achievement for them is redefined in terms of popularity and physical attractiveness. They struggle with the need for recognition through scholastic achievement versus recognition through social accomplishment.

In one woman's home, both parents were determined to prepare their daughters to take care of themselves in the face of potential difficulties. For them, educating their daughters would ensure their independence even in marriage. Their plan was to

> certainly try to find a way to send all the girls to college. The brother could probably make it on his own. The girls had to go to college. They always instilled in all of us that it was very, very important to get an education. . . . Mother fully expected that all of us were going to get married and settle down and have kids. But that we were going to be educated. She wanted us to be educated so we could be independent. (Beatrice Master, faculty)

Although the literature (Kerr, 1985) supports the need for role models and mentors for women's achievement in academe, the majority of the participants in this study were unable to establish relationships that encouraged interpersonal support. As noted by Pollard (1990), African American women administrators and faculty consistently maintain that they cannot find individuals who are interested in their research area or who are willing to work collaboratively with them. For encouragement and motivation, the women in this study relied on family members and friends as role models, especially their mothers and other mothers (Collins, 1991). They also expressed a desire to mentor other women and intentionally set up mentoring relationships. Some believed that it was their responsibility to mentor and to serve as role models.

> I mean my secretary teases me and says she's gonna hang a shingle out there because if I was charging for the number of hours that I spend counseling women and talking to them I'd be rich. But, you know, over my life I've got things from people. I have been a beneficiary without a clear distinction to say, well, I'll give you this today and I'll give you that. Somehow it worked out over the time. So I feel that I have a debt that I have to pay back. (Alicia Chambers, administrator)

One participant spoke of the affirmation she received in watching a young woman whom she mentored apply for graduate school:

> And really, just the whole process of her getting to be a senior and now applying to graduate school and how good that makes me feel to see that happen. To write that letter. That's the kind of stuff that, that's one example of the kind of things that If

find very affirming. So I don't really look to my colleagues. I look to things that I think are important and worth doing. And a lot of it does grow from my experiences. (Annette Cyrus, faculty)

For several participants, there were no clear distinctions between race and gender's affect on achievement. They found that both gender discrimination and racism had been barriers to their achievement in academia. These observations are consistent with the findings of Wilson (1989), who observed that sex discrimination has inhibited women of color's ability to achieve parity in academic administration; it is also consistent with Graves's (1990) description of African American women as victims of double jeopardy. She argued that racism and sexism have an adverse effect on their retention, promotion, and tenure:

I think . . . racism is clearly a barrier. Sexism is a barrier. You have the double whammy. I mean there have been times when I think that there was a position which I clearly was qualified for and was interested in and I didn't, I wasn't considered at all or I wasn't given adequate consideration. Or there are times when you know the only reason why people are asking you if you're interested is they want to check their affirmative action boxes. And you knew that. You can figure it out by the amount of information they send you about it. It is not enough information to make a decision. So that's been clearly a barrier. (Alicia Chambers, administrator)

National Policies and Trends

In this category, the participants described how the civil rights movement, the feminist movement, and affirmative action programs influenced their development and achievement. The social climate of the 1960s and 1970s promoted various changes in higher education. Special recruitment and admission policies were established in many institutions that traditionally had excluded Blacks. For the first time, the Executive Order outlawed sex discrimination in all federally financed employment (Chamberlain, 1989). Colleges and universities were now forced to hire women and minorities. Many of the participants were directly affected by many of these policies and trends. As students they were recruited heavily to attend prestigious schools, they were involved in consciousness-raising sessions that affected their political views, and later many of their first career appointments were as affirmative action hirees.

In many of the jobs I've had over the years, I believed I was an affirmative action hiree. I have no problem with that. Many of my students would say things like, "I don't want anybody hiring me because I'm Black. I don't care. Hire me if I can do the job. Don't hire me if I can't do the job. But give me an opportunity to prove that I can do the job. I think affirmative action is mandatory, because there is no way for us to overcome the bias that is intrinsic in this system. I have benefited greatly from it, and I'm a firm believer in it. I'm not one of these people who benefited and say, okay that's enough. It can't possibly be enough. (Paula Clark, faculty)

Another participant believed that because of affirmative action hiring practices, she was given the opportunity to function in a system that traditionally hired few African Americans:

I still think that the focus on diversity and affirmative action were responsible for me getting my foot in the door at the University of California. I still think that. I don't see it as a negative. I see it as an opportunity. But I still think that's in part why I had initial value. I've worked hard for the university and have established my work in other ways, but my first appointment was when the campus decided that it didn't have enough African Americans, so they were going to go look for them. I wasn't even job hunting when they came to me. So I think that's a national trend that has made a lot of difference. (Alicia Chambers, administrator)

Support Networks

In this category, the expectations of parents, the encouraging comments of teachers, the competitiveness of peers, and the general support of the community all influenced the participants' educational goals and occupational achievements. The participants observed their parents' expectations in their daily activities, diligent work habits, and disciplined lifestyles. These were interpreted as examples of their parents' value for education and achievement and were instrumental in the participants internalizing these values.

The literature in the area of women's achievement suggests the importance of parental nurturing and expectations. O'Donnell and Andersen (1978) reported that women in nontraditional occupations received higher expectations from their parents in terms of educational attainment and occupational involvement. Reeder and Conger (1984) observed that for Black women, their mother's occupational and parental expectations were most important. Burlew (1982) found that mothers of Black college females pursuing nontraditional careers for women were better educated, worked in nontraditional fields themselves, had early work experience, were more confident in their own ability to complete nontraditional educational programs, and had less traditional views about appropriate roles for women than traditionals. Their daughters were more likely to pursue nontraditional fields such as science, engineering, pre-law, and business, as opposed to the traditional fields of teaching, social work, and nursing.

Although the participants in this study were nurtured and supported by their parents, their experiences differed from those described in the above literature. Differences were noted in the educational and vocational levels of the parents. The majority of the parents in this study were not college graduates nor did they work in nontraditional fields. Twenty percent of the mothers finished high school, compared to 26% of the fathers. Twenty-five percent of the mothers completed college or had some college experience, compared to 16 percent of the fathers. Fifty-five percent of the mothers did not complete high school, compared to 58% of the fathers.

> My dad only had a 4th or 5th grade education. My mother probably an 8th grade. But they definitely valued education. . . . I can't recall anyone saying you got to do this or you will do this. It was an understood thing. (Carolyn Johnson, faculty)

Church

Scholars (Lincoln & Mamiya, 1990; Paris, 1985) of African American history, culture, and religion maintain that Black people uniquely and distinctively create cultures and world views that parallel the Eurocentric perspective rather than replicate the culture of which they are unvoluntary members. The Black church is one such unique form of culture. Historically, it was the only stable and coherent institution coming out of slavery. Frazier and Lincoln (1974) described the Black church as a "nation within a nation" (p. 35). The church has influenced the development of schools, banks, insurance companies, and low-income housing. Because it is also an arena of political activism, it has produced politicians-counselors and presidential candidates.

> The church was the focus of our religious life, and also the focus of all of the civic kinds of responsibilities. The civil rights movement and all of the activities taking place during this era as I was growing up had their roots in the church. (Kimberley Brown, administrator).

> I was the daughter of a minister. So I went to church three days a week. . . . From those experiences, there was often encouragement of recognition of the importance of education. That education was almost next to God in terms of its value for men, in my mind. Even if it wasn't said, they were constantly telling me how important it was in other ways. (Tonya Fletcher, administator)

As one of the more stable institutions in the Black community, the church has been recognized for its ability to develop leaders. Several participants recalled that

> [The church] taught leadership skills. I was the president of youth groups, attended vacation Bible school and Sunday school, and even taught Sunday school classes. I was also a member of the Baptist Training Union. (Esther Long, administrator)

One participant observed that

> The church has always been a strong force [in my life]. It uses the talent of young people and forces you to mold your life very early. (Alicia Chambers, administrator).

As a sanctuary, the church offered praise and a place of refuge for those attempting to escape a hostile environment and support for those seeking to survive within such an environment. Several women credit the the church as nurturing and encouraging their achievements.

> The church played a very intricate part [in my life]. At a very young age, we went to Sunday school (all of us). And you didn't go to Sunday school not knowing your lesson. You could stand up and articulate with the best of them. You got stroked for it. Amen Amen.
>
> As I grew up in the church, more and more responsibility was thrust on me. I was an associate teacher of the Sunday school class and junior church president. I was sent away to conferences. You got to shine in terms of teaching and leadership skills. Standing in front of the church presenting, if I forgot my speech, people would coach me and encourage me, saying, "Oh you know it. You can do it." My mother would rehearse me. This is how I got interested in education.
>
> Eventually, I became the secretary of the church and taught Sunday school. I got interesting in teaching; I got interesting in working with young minds. The church was the foundation from which teaching came. It was the inspiration for me to go to school and feel confident, because I could stand up in front of a crowd.
>
> I sang in the choir. My minister would say, "If you write words to a song, I'll put music to it." I would write songs, so I could say that the choir sang my song. I don't recall ever being recognized by the school. I do recall the church praising me, even for grades. "Our Betty," they would say. (Elizabeth Allen, faculty)

Another participant fondly remembers her first job as the church organist, which provided much-needed income for the family.

> I started playing the piano and was a musician by the age of 10, working in my local chuch. I was playing the piano. By the time I was 14, I was the church organist, because they asked me if I would like to learn. They paid for me to have lessons on the organ so that I could play, and that was how I helped to supplement my parents' income. My income. I didn't get an allowance. So it was the only money that I had to live on. (Annette Cyrus, faculty)

Some of the participants continued their involvement in the church into adulthood. One maintains that she and her siblings are active members in their local congregation.

> It has been a big part of our lives. All of us, all four of us, are still very active in our churches. (Beatrice Masters, administrator)

She also expressed her appreciation for the church and its teachings about money and stewardship.

> [M]oney, not so much as a dominant feature, but a recognition that you had to be a good steward of your money, partially from the religious tradition, too . . . a sense that you have a willingness to share. Generosity is a value . . . a sense that somehow, for some reason you don't quite understand, you've been given a little bit more than other people and so you have a responsibility to give something back.

Personal Beliefs

In this category, participants described how they make meaning out of their lives. They began by having a sense of purpose and believing that one must define her calling and the depth of her commitment to others. They also discussed the motivation to achieve, not as a mere act in itself but as a service to others or a higher self. "I am motivated by own passion about . . . having a real impact on . . . people's lives."

Their driving force or source of motivation is grounded in their personality characteristics: Perseverance—"I grew up recognizing that if I set a course and kept at it and worked hard I would achieve." Determination—"Well I'm not a loser, so whether or not I saw it being the experience I thought it was going to be, I made it that." Tenacity—"I am a tenacious person. I don't see obstacles." Discipline—"There's no such thing as a lucky break. You have to work so that when the break happens you're ready for it."

Escapism

A strong desire to escape poor living conditions motivated the participants in this category to achieve. Their ultimate escape plan involved hard work, voracious reading, and the acceptance that individuals have choices. The participants vowed to create a better life for themselves. They decided that an education would lead them to financial stability, better housing, and better working conditions.

I had this real strong drive to get out of something. I keep remembering it. I remember saying things like this would never do. Or, maybe I would be going to the store and I would have this experience with wild dogs; or going to school and these dogs were chasing me, I had to jump up on this car and tore my new little dress. I remember hearing these mangy-looking rabid dogs, and I'm on top of this little funky car, saying this is not going to make it here. We've got to do something more than this girl. Or, maybe a couple of times, when I was in near-assault situations, where someone was trying to rob me or get me into their car. I remember thinking, I am too young for this. Like here I am nine years old, having to deal with these issues. What's wrong with this picture ? I have a lot of those kinds of questions in my head, saying, I can't hang with this. Or, watching my girlfriends and their lives kind of self-destruct. Watching these parents treat their kids like crap. I remember thinking, I am not going to choose this. I am going to do something different. I didn't know what that was. (Dionne Christian, administrator)

Reflections

A critical examination of the six categories reveals the importance of racial and gender identity, community support, national policies and trends, and a strong sense of efficacy. These themes are significant for the achievement of African American women faculty and administrators in higher education. They encouraged the participants in this study to survive the multiple barriers of discrimination in higher education. Implanting these strategies will transform other higher education institutions into multicultural environments.

Racial and Gender Identity

Parental support was significant in the development of the participants' strong racial and gender identity. Early in the participants' lives, their parents' primary goal was to prepare the participants to survive in a racist society. The parents' prevailing message about racial identity was that despite obstacles or difficulties, the participant was expected to work hard to achieve.

Parental support also evident in shaping the participants' identity as females. In preparation for life in a sexist society, participants were taught that they could control their lives. The mothers' expectations influenced the attitudes, behaviors, and experiences of the participants. They taught their daughters that their decisions and actions would determine which goals they could attain.

Community Support

Community support was a significant factor in African American women's achievement in academe. It established a supportive environment that functioned as an extended family: "I was the neighborhood's child." "Every mother was my mother." The participants received support and encouragement from: teachers ("All of the teachers in the school really helped and encouraged me."); peers ("As I've grown older, I have come to understand that it was only after they believed in me, I began to believe in myself."); and the church ("The church taught me leadership skills." "It has been a strong force in my life."). Results from this study indicate that achievement is even more likely to occur when the individual is a member of a larger supportive environment.

National Policies and Trends

National policies and trends enhanced the achievement of African American women faculty and administrators. The majority of the women in this study grew up in working-class families. Although education and achievement were valued by the family, many of the participants would not have been able to attend college without the assistance of scholarships and special admissions programs.

Affirmative action programs were also significant for the participants' achievements. The programs offered many of the women the opportunity to achieve. National policies are needed to ensure that African American women faculty and administrators can achieve. Without these policies, many of the women in this study would not have made the exemplary contributions they have to society and to higher education. Their achievements also counteract the popular belief that affirmative action programs hire unqualified minorities. As stated by several of the participants, all they wanted was an opportunity to prove that they "could do the job."

Self-Efficacy

A strong sense of efficacy sustained the women in their efforts to respond to racial and gender discrimination, economic disparity, and legal segregation. A strong sense of efficacy enabled the participants to persevere to overcome obstacles and reach their goals. They were confident in their judgments to execute the necessary courses of action required for their achievement. According to Bandura (1986), "high perseverance usually produces high performance attainments" (p. 123). The women's strong sense of efficacy was probably influenced by the collective efficacy of the family, the community, and the church, all necessary for their achievement in academe.

REFERENCES

Allen, L., & Majidi-Ahi, S. (1989). Black American children. In J. T. Gibbs, L. N. Huang, & Associates (Eds.), *Children of color* (pp. 148–178). San Francisco: Jossey-Bass.

Astin, W. (1982). *Minorities in Americas' higher education.* San Francisco: Jossey-Bass.

Bandura, A. (1986). *Social foundations of thought and action: A social cognitive theory.* Englewood Cliffs, NJ: Prentice Hall.

Betz, N., & Fitzgerald, L. (1987). *The career psychology of women.* Orlando: Academic Press.

Blackwell, J. (1991). *The Black community.* New York: Harper Collins.

Burlew, A. K. (1982). The experiences of black females in traditional and nontraditional professions. *Psychology of Women Quarterly, 6*(3), 313–327.

Cannon, K. (1985). The emergence of a Black feminist consciousness. In L. M. Russell (Ed.), *Feminist interpretations of the Bible* (pp. 30–40). Philadelphia: Westminister Press.

Carter, D., Pearson, C., & Shavlik, D. (Eds.). (1987/1988). Double jeopardy: Women of color. *Higher Educational Record, 68,* 98–103.

Chamberlain, M. (1989). *Women in academe: Progress and prospects.* New York: Russell Sage Foundation.

Collins, P. (1991). *Black feminist thought: Knowledge, consciousness, and the politics of empowerment.* New York: Routledge Press.

Elam, J. (1989). *Blacks in higher education: Overcoming the odds.* New York: University Press of America.

Farmer, H. (1985). Model of career and achievement motivation for women and men. *Journal of Counseling Psychology, 32*(3), 363–390.

Fassinger, R. E. (1985). A causal model of career choice in college women. *Journal of Vocational Behavior, 27,* 123–153.

Finkelstein, M. (1985). *The American academic profession: A synthesis of social scientific inquiry since World War II.* Columbus: Ohio State University Press.

Fleming, J., Gill, G., & Swinton, D. (1978). *The case for affirmative action for Blacks in higher education.* Washington, DC: Institute for the Study of Educational Policy, Howard University Press.

Frazier, E. F., & Lincoln, C. E. (1974). *The Negro church in America/The Black church since Frazier.* New York: Schocken Books.

Gilbert, L. A. (1985). Measures of psychological masculiniy and femininity: A comment on Gadd, Glass, and Arnkoff. *Journal of Counseling Psychology, 32,* 163–166.

Gilligan, C. (1990). *Making connections: The relational world of adolescent girls at Emma Willard School.* Cambridge: Harvard University Press.

Graves, S. (1990). A case of double jeopardy? Black women in higher education. *Initiatives, 53,* 1–8.

Hamilton, K. (1971). *Goals and plans of Black women.* New York: Exposition Press.

Hensel, N. (1991). *Realizing gender equality in higher education: The need to integrate work/family issues.* Washington, DC: Clearinghouse on Higher Education. (ASHE-ERIC Higher Education Report 2.

Hooks, B., & West, C. (1991). *Breaking bread: Insurgent Black intellectual life.* Boston: South End Press.

Kerr, B. (1985). *Smart girls, gifted women.* Columbus, OH: Psychology Press.

Lincoln, C. E., & Mamiya, L. (1990). *The Black church in the African American experience.* Durham: Duke University Press.

McAdoo, H. (1988). *Black families.* Newbury Park, CA: Sage Publications.

Menges, R., & Exum, W. (1983). Barriers to the progress of women and minority faculty. *Journal of Higher Education, 54*(2), 123–143.

Mosley, M. (1980). Black women administrators in higher education: An endangered species. *Journal of Black Studies, 10*(3), 295–310.

Murray, S. R. Who is that person? Images and roles of Black women. In S. Cox (Ed.), *Female psychology—The emerging self* (2d ed., pp. 113–123). New York: St. Martin's Press.

O'Donnell, J., & Andersen, D. (1978). Factors influencing choice of major and career of capable women. Vocational Guidance Quarterly, 26, 214–221.

Paris, P. J. (1985). *The social teaching of the Black churches.* Philadelphia: Fortress Press.

Pollard, D. (1990). Black women, interpersonal support, and institutional change. In J. Antler & S. Biklen (Eds.), *Changing education: Women as radicals and conservators.* Albany: State University Press of New York.

Reeder, A., & Conger, R. (1984). Differential mother and father influences on the educational attainment of Black and white women. *The Sociological Quarterly, 25,* 239–250.

Sadker, M., & Sadker, D. (1994). *Failing at fairness: How America's schools cheat girls.* New York: Charles Scribner's Sons.

Smith, E. (1985). Upward mobility: Black and white women administrators. *Journal of NAWDAC, 52,* 28–32.

Strauss, A., & Corbin, J. (1990). *Basics of qualitative research. Grounded theory procedures and techniques.* Newbury Park, CA: Sage Publications.

Swann, R., & Witty, E. (1980). Black women administrators at traditionally Black colleges and universities: Attitudes, perceptions, and potentials. *Western Journal of Black Studies, 4,* 261–270.

Theodore, A. (1986). *The campus troublemakers: Academic women in protest.* Houston: Cap and Gown Press.

Tinsley, A., Secor, C., & Kaplan, S. (Eds.). (1984). *New directions for higher education: Women in higher education administration.* San Francisco: Jossey-Bass.

Touchton, J., & Davis, L. (1991). Fact book on American women in higher education. New York: Council on Education, Macmillan.

Washington, V., & Harvey, W. (1989). *Affirmative rhetoric, negative action: African American and Hispanic faculty at predominantly white institutions.* Washington, DC: Clearinghouse on Higher Education. (ASHE-ERIC Higher Education Report 2.

Williams, A. (1989). Research on Black women college administrators: Descriptive and interview data. *Sex Roles, 21,* 99–112.

Wilson, K. L. (1987). Explaining the educational attainment of young Black adults: Critical familial and extra-familial influences. *Journal of Negro Education, 56*(1), 64–76.

Wilson, R. (1989). Women of color in academic administration: Trends, progress, and barriers. *Sex Roles, 21,* 85–97.

PART IV

Student Perspective

Five Recommendations to Build a Multicultural Campus

Graduate Student
Abayomi Adejokun

- The university/college must *recruit* and *retain* minority faculty who are committed to mentoring graduate students, especially students of color.

- The college/department leadership must actively *promote* their interest in students of color (for example, meeting personally with students several times a year).

- Departments must *encourage* and *support* changes in the curriculum, reflecting new experiences and perspectives of diverse groups.

- Programs must *expand* the focus of research to include topics that are nontraditional in American higher education (for example, a case study of institutional racism within the college).

- Departments must *recognize* and *accept* publications in ethnically oriented journals.

Nine

An African Student's View of Educational Leadership

Aggressive, ambitious, intelligent, creative, and loaded with leadership potential. These are the words that Ms. Grant, my 10th-grade social studies teacher, used to describe me in a letter of recommendation to a potential employer. Not surprisingly, such flattering accolades resulted in a job offer. I remember this because it was my first paid employment.

Two years later, at my graduation, Ms. Grant walked up to me, gave me a brisk hug and said, "Well, you're on your way to college now, perhaps you should consider becoming an educator. You could make an impact on students in a very special way." Until then, I never considered a career as an educator, let alone as an educational leader. At the time, I had no idea what Ms. Grant meant when she said, "You could make an impact in a very special way." Though it was clear that Ms. Grant held me in high regard, the voice and context in which she spoke was unfamiliar to me. In retrospect, I realize she meant that if I nurtured the promising talent and ambition she saw in me, I could become a serious contributor to the field of education. I did not, however, become interested in education until well into my college years, and even then, I subconsciously resisted the idea. I did so because I perceived the professional educator as a "sitting duck" for parents, central administration, taxpayers, and various advocacy groups to attack at their will.

My view of educational leadership was clear and simple. I saw it a profession fraught with bureaucracy, midcareer disenchantment, anxiety, and stress, all of which culminate in burnout. Consequently, after graduating from college, I asked myself the following questions. Why should I settle for an average job that doesn't require much of me? Why should I take away time from my family and expand my workday from 8 hours a day to 10 or 12? Why should I take on a role that is inherently political, stress ridden, and thankless in many ways? Why would I take on a role that might subject me to being vilified anytime I made hard decisions that translated into a loss for some and a gain for others? Why risk the loss of friendship and fellowship of my colleagues or those whom I lead? In short, who needs the aggravation?

The incentives for being an educational leader these days seem to be diminishing rapidly. Not only are accomplishments not as handsomely rewarded as they once were, but reports of in-fighting seem to be on the increase and advancement on the decrease. In his report on corporate managers and academicians, Michael Maccoby (1976) said of academia: "If corporate managers engaged in the nit-picking and down-putting common in universities, little would be created and produced. If managers treated their subordinates with the neglect and contempt common in the attitudes of professors, no one would work for them. These days, the talented jungle fighter probably has a much better chance for advancement in the university than in the corporate psychostructure" (p. 209).

Over a decade later, similar problems still exist, but in a new dimension. John Holcomb (1987) indicated that many of the people who should be training to become society's next leaders simply aren't interested. The field of education doesn't offer any real financial incentives. He contends that graduate students earn more per hour as classroom teachers than they would as principals, once the extra hours on the job are considered. With the increasing complexity of today's educational issues, educators must spend more time at the office and less time at home. And, more than at any other time, educational leaders are thought to have too much power and authority. Therefore, they are challenged first by their staff, then by their superiors, and finally by the public-at-large. Soon they are left with less-than-adequate decision-making power or authority to respond meaningfully to the needs and goals of the organization.

Many of these problems exist in other fields. For example, business and industry are notorious for having bright and potential leaders who choose to stay in the safety of the herd rather than strive for a vulnerable leadership position. They do this by citing security, friendship, and a dozen other familiar reasons. There is an endless supply of excuses for those who want to avoid challenges. Some reasons are generated from research questionnaires and others come from personal beliefs and convictions.

At first the more I thought about it, the more I was able to justify not becoming an educational leader. Then I became aware that I was doing several things to stifle my growth, both personally and professionally. I decided to turn my attitude and thinking around. Finally, I came to the realization that to abdicate one's sense of civic duty to contribute to community, betterment of life, and the cultivation of an excellent learning environment was to be apathetic, unresponding, and negligent.

Although life has no guarantees, one thing is certain: For people who are ready to stand up and be counted as leaders, there are incentives that cannot be measured by money or amount of leisure time. The glow on a student's face when he or she fully understands a concept; the pride and confidence that faculty get when they are pushed to intellectually develop themselves beyond their dreams; and the feeling of accomplishment when a successful program benefits communities—these are all invaluable and intangible reasons for becoming an educational leader.

Many scholars agree that the paramount goal of any educational leader is to assume clear, articulate, and forceful leadership in defining the role of the school. This is done to accomplish an even larger goal—the provision of equal and quality education to all students. Somehow, the educational enterprise as a whole has fallen short of this achievable goal. Instead, quality education, regardless of race and social class, is still a goal that's given lip service by "silver-tongued do-nothing conformists" rather than being propelled by positive action. James Cheek, a former president of Howard University, said it best when he suggested that "social justice is just an empty phrase without the leadership committed to the fulfillment of the idea" (used in Scott, 1975). In simple terms, those who wish to be or are educational leaders must believe that educators—regardless of race, gender, or ethnicity—have a supreme obligation to use their position to eradicate racism and socioeconomic inequities. By the same token, they must recognize and withstand negative internal and external forces that control their ability to be effective and successful (Scott, 1990).

Not long ago, President Bill Clinton suggested that strong leaders create strong schools. The state of our educational system is proof that we are in need of strong educational leaders to pilot the course for our schools and to ensure quality education. Leaders who are dynamic in nature, who are willing to throw themselves into a relationship with followers, will feel elevated to the point that they become catalysts for change, thereby creating a new category of leaders. The time has come for leaders in education to gather the skills to understand and promote boldness over softness, creativity instead of rigidity. In plain terms, we want men and women who are up to the challenge, fearless in their pursuits, and willing to lead the way.

Deep Water, Short Breath: Meeting the Challenges of the Twenty-First Century

In the past, men and women of different racial and ethnic backgrounds have answered the call for needed educational leadership with some success. Most notable in this regard is that institutions of higher education in this country are no longer private ivy-covered domains reserved for white males (Bauer, 1988). Gone are the days when the unspoken assumption was that the education of white students should be undertaken, for the most part, in isolation from students of color (Kinnick, 1994). Gone are the days when the education of African Americans was vigilantly withheld and there were stiff legal consequences against those who dared challenge exclusionary policies. For the most part, higher education has become less elitist, more democratic, more accessible, less homogeneous, and less overtly discriminatory (Kinnick, 1994). However, in broader scope, the combination of evolving societal trends, cancerous effects of racism, and socioeconomic inequalities have begun to diminish progress made in past decades. Circumstances cited below highlight the problems facing minorities in higher education:

* African Americans continue to be the most underrepresented group at most predominantly white four-year institutions and often lack the mentorship and guidance needed to complete their programs with few problems.

* The attrition rates for African Americans and Hispanics in higher education are roughly twice those of whites.

- African American, Hispanic, and Native American participation in graduate and professional schools remains exceptionally low.

- The percentage of minorities taking college preparatory classes in high school is on the decline.

- More states are using standard performance tests to set graduation standards for students. Due to cultural differences and historically inferior education, African Americans and Hispanics tend to do poorly on these tests.

- More college graduates face unemployment and are frustrated by the perceived inability of educational institutions to prepare them for the real world. (Scott, 1990)

To reverse this course, many scholars have a collective perception that, by and large, minority administrators best serve the educational demands of a culturally pluralistic society when they significantly shape policies and control how such policies are executed (Bowen, 1993; Dawson-Lovelady, 1981; Herbert, 1974). They understand the magnitude and nature of the problems confronting people from historically marginalized groups. This point further suggests that, culturally, some African Americans develop an empathetic attitude toward exploited people and an interest in establishing equity, care, and cooperation (Astin, 1992).

Based on the premise that some African Americans tend to bring a vision of leadership that stresses inclusiveness and more cultural and ethnic balance, it is easy to understand that moral obligation would include the recruitment and retention of minority faculty. It would also nurture the progress of all students, particularly students of color.

African Americans are drawn from a diverse range of cultures and countries, first from Africa and later from the Caribbean and Central and South America. We all share the history of enslavement, acculturation, and racial oppression that gives relevance to the initial bond of African heritage. Being African American in America means not only being racially and culturally different, it also means being treated as inferior by most white Americans (Scott, 1994). Africans and African Americans are intricately linked in origin, ancestry, and spirit. With such a linkage, Africans are subjected to the same prejudices and discrimination that impede African Americans. Therefore, I, an African, share the African American commitment to lift up the historically disenfranchised members of this society.

Tony Brown, a nationally syndicated radio talk show host, suggested that, "although America offers many people opportunities that they may not otherwise have anywhere else in the world, foreigners who choose to immigrate into this country, in search of the new and brighter opportunity it offers, must be prepared to burden the effects of the racist and ethnocentric beliefs that are attached with such opportunities" (CSPAN; July 17, 1996).

Hence, in the spirit of brotherhood, I, an African who is aspiring to become an educational leader, have pledged allegiance to the same concerns that African American educational leaders have. Those concerns are as follows: equitable recruitment, promotion, and tenure of minority faculty; inclusion of minority faculty in mainstream research; support for the continual development of minority faculty through sabbaticals, workshops, conferences, and symposia; cultivation of breadth; support for minority-focused research; mentorships and directorships for new faculty (especially those who want to go into administration); recruitment of academically talented, but disadvantaged minority students (graduate and undergraduate); financial support for economically disadvantaged students (both white and minorities); employment policies and practices that will provide better access for African American faculty members; and the formation of solid relationships with surrounding African American communities. All are factors that can significantly improve students' education, especially students of color.

African American educational leaders at my school are aware of the disparities in hiring, tenure, and promotion (the "good old boy system"). They support the overall growth and progress of African Americans and other minority groups and, thus, pledge allegiance to promoting equality for these groups. They do so because all of them have experienced racism and are familiar with the challenges of climbing the academic ladder. For example, one administrator testified that in the beginning of his academic career he was considered incompetent and his qualifications were minimized because his critics preferred a white individual for the position. In addition, his scholarship was deemed unimportant and an aberration from mainstream research issues because it centered on African American issues. In another situation, an African American administrator was consistently passed over for promotion in spite of his productivity and seniority in the department.

African American administrators understand that, for the most part, predominantly white institutions are reluctant or unwilling to embrace the minority experience. "Diversity on most campuses is still measured by numbers and percentages rather than by revising the map of the white majority's intellectual terrain" (Scott, 1990, p. 63). Thus, for many African American educators, their beliefs and decisions on issues of equity and pluralism are affected not only by sociological values, but also by their familiarity with the problems and needs of majority and minority group members. Hence, the African American educational leader's priorities and strategies are derived from his or her beliefs and principal educational assumptions.

Relating this theory to leadership, the two most basic, yet difficult, questions for these African American educators are: What responsibility do I have to minority groups? What role should I play in making academia more responsive to the needs of all people? Attempting to answer these questions reveals the complexity of this issue. Because of the transformative nature of these moral obligations, educational leaders will face more challenges and hostility from their counterparts in the workplace.

The Cycle of Challenges in Educational Leadership: From Old to New

Higher education is known for its complexities, contradictions, and changing traditions. Amid such chaos, African American educational leaders must operate with the challenges associated with their race. This situation is most noticeable for African American administrators who work in predominantly white settings. Scott (1975) noted that "African American school administrators are rarely permitted by whites or African Americans to function as educational leader, whose race is incidental to his expertise and performance" (p. 437). In spite of the knowledge, commitment, and vision they bring to college campuses, the African American educational leader's effort is continually affected by the multifaceted barriers uniquely linked to society's treatment of African Americans.

From the start, African American educators have faced the ironic situation of having impressive titles but no corresponding power and the feeling that they acquired their jobs not through skill or impressive work history, but because of affirmative action. There are two consequences to this. First, it frustrates their ability to act meaningfully on behalf of minority students. Second, any opportunity to respond to the concerns of minority students is usually dictated by white school officials, who are less affected by the decisions they make. These problems have existed since African Americans arrived at predominantly white institutions. Unfortunately, these age-old problems have been transformed and have emerged as new-age problems.

As a student in the educational leadership field, I am faced with the new-age challenges that many of my predecessors encountered earlier. A classic example occurred when a professor encouraged me to take his leadership course. Thinking I could only gain more useful knowledge about leadership, I agreed to drop the class I was enrolled in to take this highly advertised class. As the class began, we were introduced to various leadership theorists from Machiavelli to current management theorists such as Tom Peters and the like.

Though it was worthwhile to discuss these European leaders' ideologies, it was only useful to a point. The usefulness was limited because none of the European theorists spoke about the leadership of people of color, which was outside of their experiences. Thus, I had very limited exposure to leaders who came from and had different perspectives. The fact is, African Americans, Hispanics, and Native American leaders face diametrically different issues when leading (Scott, 1994). This point is more valid in cases where the leader is of a different race than that to which his or her followers belong (for example, African American administrators in predominantly white institutions).

Being an aspiring leader who is African, I wanted to know of the struggles, challenges, and triumphs of African American leaders who came before me. I wanted to gain a deeper understanding of the issues and leadership strategies I may need to adopt as an African American leader. I decided to ask the professor why African Americans were not part of the learning experiences and curriculum in his leadership class. With a bewildered look on his face he replied, "African American leaders do not exist in scholarly journals that matter." Then, with an equally perplexed look on my face, I responded, "You mean to tell me that people like Dr. Martin Luther King, Ralph Abernathy, Frederick Douglas, Malcom X, and General Colin Powell do not exist in literature? Why, tons of books and articles have been published about these people and others like them." Aware of the lack of substance of his excuse, he simply shrugged his shoulders and walked off. Little did I know then that he was greatly offended by my inquiry, which he considered an arrogant challenge to his expertise. Since that day, he has seen me as an enemy.

The significance of this situation is that, historically, African American administrators in predominantly white institutions have been systematically and overtly isolated from involvement in institutional decisions as they relate to minority students (Grace, 1988). Today, minorities are often excluded from the curriculum by rationalizing the opposing evidence and conforming to preexisting beliefs. African American leaders' involvement in various segments of higher education (that is, curriculum, administration, decision-making processes) may also be limited by simplifying, distorting, or rejecting facts (Adejokun, 1997).

In the example I gave above, the professor's response reflects the history of institutions of higher education. Such actions have consciously limited the quality of education given to people of color. Introducing and discussing the experiences and perspectives of European males only, while ignoring all other relevant perspectives, devalues the contributions of others. Many students of color have decided to challenge the ways teaching and learning have traditionally taken place at our institutions. To do this, we look at the contradictions of various viewpoints and introduce new information and concepts that are relevant to our cultural backgrounds. All too often, taking such a stand can create conflict and animosity between faculty and students. Conflict is an inescapable characteristic of human interaction. Using conflict to create a forum for discussion offers a great opportunity to turn things around. Noonan's (1988) observation speaks to this issue, stating, "unacknowledged, the conflict between not wanting to upset others and wanting to pursue truth can silence students and faculty" (p. 83).

Another dimension of the new-aged problems that I face as an aspiring African American educational leader is controversy concerning the focus of my research. More often than not, African Americans focus on topics surrounding the current state of African Americans educationally, socially, psychologically, and professionally—and for good reason. A few of the urgent issues focusing on African Americans are the overrepresentation of African American males in prison; the increasing number of African American students being systematically and uncaringly deemed as unmotivated and subsequently placed in special education classes; the declining number of African Americans going to and graduating from college; and the extremely low number of African American faculty receiving promotion or tenure.

Increasing numbers of minority faculty continue to report that they feel unappreciated and unsupported in their departments and that their research is often devalued and viewed as peripheral (Rothblum, 1988). In fact, minority faculty receive criticism from both faculty members and administration. Minority faculty claim that university administrations are critical, unaccepting, and tend to withhold resources because they were considered "ghetto disciplines," worthy of publication only in what they deem as inferior, ethnically oriented journals (Bronstein, 1993). The controversy surrounding our research topics has greater implications than that it is academically one dimensional in focus, which is the most common criticism and what I consider to be the harshest. Much of the research on such issues is scholarly and morally worthy. The criticism itself is shallow and lacks substantive evidence supporting its position.

The sad reality is that a good deal of the hostility and academic damnation directed toward faculty of color is not only at the professorial level; it also extends to students. If people can be discouraged from doing research on African American issues during their student years, a critical time for career decisions, they will be less likely to pursue such issues when they join the professional ranks.

My experience as a student has been to engage in topics important to African Americans and the improvement of their education. I am often approached by people whom I refer to as "do-gooders." These people are eager to give advice as to what direction they think I should go in my research to produce a more meaningful study. Though I value good advice as any academician should, much of the advice I get attempts to steer my focus away from its original intent. For example, it is not uncommon for me to begin by thinking about doing a study of the "academic achievements of gifted African American students in college." After a series of suggestions from do-gooders, the focus ends up being something like "the effects of single parenting on gifted African American students." The latter topic is one that changes focus from an issue that could potentially motivate, uplift, and restore the self-esteem of other African American and minority students. Instead, it reminds African American youth of the harsh and dismal situation they are confronted with, thus creating self-doubt, lack of confidence, and lack of ability to overcome such obstacles.

Many of the do-gooders operate unconsciously within the established norm. That is, they tend to report negative information regarding minority student's lives, particularly African Americans and Hispanic Americans. More often than not, the literature pertaining to these two groups reflect negative issues such as behavioral problems, lower achievement scores, low retention rates, and lower standards in general. Therefore, when a change in direction is initiated, there is a tendency to revert back to the way things have historically been done. I have found it of critical importance to acquire the skills to be open and receptive to the advice of others, while balancing the need to be true to my original ideas. This means that students have to be able to filter information, deciphering what is and is not useful.

Black Knights, White Fortress

We are close to the twenty-first century, yet there has been no significant change in the number of African Americans in upper-level administration. The scant number of high-level African American administrators has, in part, slowed the pace of progress in regard to what can be accomplished through diversity in higher education. However, in spite of their low numbers, African American educational leaders have made some strides through their unrelenting efforts. They have done this by standing up to unfair academic practices that impose inequitable burdens on African Americans and other minority students.

In a white-dominated society, African Americans have high unemployment rates, inferior occupational distributions, low wages and earnings, and a high probability of being the last hired and the first fired. They are subjected to long-standing educational and employment discrimination, are the last to be given tenure or promotion, and are the first whose work and research is devalued and mocked. Given this, African American administrators are Black Knights seeking survival and success in a White Fortress.

Their struggles in predominantly white institutions have brought them some degree of success and survival, but much of it came with a price. Many have encountered problems such as having their qualifications minimized, having their credibility challenged, and being labeled incompetent (Adejokun, 1997). Their measure of success has benefited not only African American students, but Hispanic Americans, Native Americans, and Asian American students as well. Their presence has provided us with much needed scholarship and mentorship and has instilled in us a sense of self-confidence. But most importantly, African American educational leaders have been our "academic attorneys," standing firm to ensure that we receive equality, fairness, and due process as we walk the halls of academia.

They have been watchdog groups who have stood guard for minorities by interpreting and advising them on institutional policies and instructing them on how to use these policies to their advantage. This point was certainly corroborated in my conversation with an African American dean in a predominantly white institution. He said that, in his opinion, African American students had to be the African American version of Einstein to gain admission to his institution. After a series of stringent requirements, the students who made it were often subjected to covert hostile and unfair treatment—a practice that does not resemble how the majority of white students are treated during the admission process.

This is just one more reminder of the privileges available to the majority group. This privileged treatment helps whites excel and produce at their optimum level. This white privilege can be considered as "an invisible, weightless knapsack of special provisions, assurances, tools, maps, guides, codebooks, passports, visas, clothes, compasses, and blank checks" (McIntosh, 1988, p. 2). The dean suggested that at the point when privileges are given to some and denied to others, he consciously polices the actions of the institution, whenever warranted. The following is an example he gave attesting to this fact:

> One Monday morning, an African American graduate student sat by the door of his office, weeping over what she deemed as an unjustified failure of her preliminary exam. She explained to the dean that she had failed and no explanation was given to her by any of the committee. The dean, remembering this student as one who was recently awarded a scholarship for maintaining a 4.0 G.P.A. since her arrival into the graduate program, invited her into his office to get more details about what transpired. On further examination, he discovered that the student was failed on the very same subject that she had taught as a teaching assistant for several semesters. Her evaluation records revealed that she was competent in the subject and her students were pleased with what they had learned. The dean, armed with this evidence, decided to speak to the committee himself. The committee responded that although she answered all other questions satisfactorily, they felt she answered the last question vaguely without the specificity they wanted. On introducing the evidence of the student's superior performance in this subject and testimonies from the student's other professors, the student was allowed to retake the exam. She scored well and passed the exam.

The dean shared with me the fact that he had observed instances when that same committee overlooked inadequate answers from white students and passed them. He ended by saying that if he had not been there to help and advocate for this student, she probably would not have been allowed to retake the exam and would have faced possible expulsion from the program. It would have been a case of "another African American student eliminated from the race to success" (Adejokun, 1997).

Whatever we choose to call them—heroes who brave the right but unpopular position, knights who protect the interests of justice, or guardian angels who look out for our best interests—one fact remains: their eternal and continual struggle to plant seeds of equity and fairness is a task to which the next generation of African American educational leaders must adhere. To ignore the shaping policies and culture that drive academia is to curse the efforts these leaders have made for the betterment of individuals and groups. And to curse their efforts is to have all students lose a friend, guidance counselor, academic adviser, job placement officer, mentor, spokesperson as well as a booster in times of trouble and a congratulator in times of success. In essence, they work relentlessly to champion our cause, paying the price even when they have nothing left to pay.

True African American educators have endured. They have brought to leadership the sum total of their unique values, sentiments, and experiences as African Americans in America. More noticeably, they have brought to our attention that just as the beauties of nature surface in all colors, so does the strength of humankind emerge in many forms. Through their combined triumphs and accomplishments, we have come to understand that all people of color are unique, and it is this uniqueness that propels us to contribution. Above all, African American educational leaders have made and continue to make their contributions, but their contributions are only as effective and lasting as much as they are consistently being built upon. In light of this, the next generation of African American educational leaders must be courageous souls driven by vision and passion to become change agents. They must shape the destinies of communities and transmit values that will improve educational opportunity and equality for all.

REFERENCES

Adejokun, A. A. (1997). *African American knights, white fortress: Perceptions and leadership strategies of African American deans in predominantly white institutions.* Unpublished dissertation. Pullman: Washington State University.

Astin, H. S. (1992). *Women of influence, Woman of vision.* San Francisco: Jossey-Bass.

Bauer, H. H. (1988). *To rise above principle: The memoirs of an unreconstructed dean.* Urbana: University of Illinois Press.

Bowen, R. (1993, May). *Vision and the African American community college president.* Conference paper presented National Association of Black School Administrators. Long Island, New York.

Bronstein, P. (1993). Challenges, rewards, and costs for feminist and ethnic minority scholars. *New Directions for Teaching and Learning, 53,* 1.

CSPAN. (1996). Tony Brown on the advancement of the upcoming generation. Washington DC.

Dawson-Lovelady, F. (1981). No room at the top: Women & minorities in education. *Principal, 61,* 37–40.

Grace, C. A. (1988). *Ethnic identity, gender and adult development as factors in the experiences of African American professionals in predominantly white institutions.* Unpublished dissertation. New York: City University of New York.

Herbert, A. (1974). The minority administrator: Problems, prospects, and challenges. *Public Administration Review, 35,* 6, 17–23.

Holcomb, H. J. (1987). Boards must urge promising young school leaders to step forward. *American School Board Journal, 174*(5), 32–33.

Kinnick, M. K (1994). *Providing useful information for deans and department chairs.* San Francisco: Jossey-Bass.

Maccoby, M. (1976). *The gamesman.* New York: Simon and Schuster.

McIntosh, P. (1988). White privilege and male privilege: A personal account of coming to see correspondences through work in women's studies (issue brief no. 189, pp. 1–2). Wellesley, MA: Center for Research on Women.

Noonan, J. F. (1988). Discussing racial topics in class. In M. Adams & L. Marchesani (Eds.), *Racial and cultural diversity, curricular content, and classroom dynamics: A manual for college teachers* (pp. 59–74). Amherst: University of Massachusetts Press.

Rothblum, E. D. (1988). Leaving the ivory tower: Factors contributing to women's voluntary resignation from academia. *Frontiers, 109*(2), 14–17.

Scott, H. J. (1975). African American consciousness and professionalism. *Journal of Negro Education, 44*(3), 432–439.

Scott, H. J. (1990). The quest for equity: Implications for administrators in higher education. *Leadership and Equity, 15,* 59–75.

Scott, H. J. (1994, November). *African Americans and the quest for equality.* A commissioned paper for the Charles Moody Institute for Research and Development. Presented at the 24th annual National Association of African American School Educators, Washington, DC.

About the Authors

ABAYOMI ADEJOKUN is currently a leadership consultant for a managment firm. He has a master's in Public Administration from Florida A & M University and received his Ph.D. in Educational Leadership from Washington State University in May 1997. Dr. Adejokun has more than eight years of corporate management experience in change management. He has also been an analyst with the Florida House of Representatives, working and consulting on education and welfare reform and corrections initiatives. Dr. Adejokun has received numerous awards, including the 1997 Distinguished Directors Award, the 1996 Merrel B. Excellence award, and an Irene Ryan nomination. He continues to travel across the country giving presentations on leadership and its impact on the interpersonal development of organizational members.

VANESSA ALLEN-BROWN is assistant professor in the College of Education at the University of Cincinnati. She received her Ph.D. in educational studies at the University of Missouri, Columbia. Some of her publications can be found in the *Journal of Peace and Change* and in educational journals. Her areas of interest include philosophy, history, Black women in education, and liberation theology.

LOUIS A. CASTENELL, JR. is dean, College of Education, University of Cincinnati. His Ph.D. is in educational psychology and was awarded by the University of Illinois, Urbana-Champaign. Dr. Castenell serves on numerous professional and civic boards and was the 1993 Critics Choice Award recipient for outstanding written contributions to an area related to Educational Studies.

A. REYNALDO CONTRERAS chairs the Department of Administrative and Inter-disciplinary Studies at San Francisco State University. Formerly, he was professor of Educational Leadership and Policy Studies at Indiana University, Bloomington. Dr. Contreras received his Ph.D. from Stanford University, where he studied administration and policy analysis. His research interests include policy studies in education, minority educational leadership, and education in emerging metropolitan contexts. He has served on editorial boards of book series and journals and has contributed to journals and books on educational leadership, educational policy, and urban education.

FLORA IDA ORTIZ is currently a professor of educational administration at the University of California, Riverside. She has written extensively on educational careers, women and minorities in education, socialization processes, and other areas in educational administration. Some of her books include *Career patterns in education: Women, men and minorities in public school administration* (1982) and, most recently, *Schoolhousing: Planning and designing educational facilities* (1994).

MYRTIS H. POWELL was appointed vice president for Student Affairs at Miami University in 1989. She had been executive assistant to the president at Miami since 1981. Dr. Powell received her B.S., M.A., and Ph.D. degrees from the University of Cincinnati. She also has a certificate in educational management from the Harvard University Graduate School of Business.

HOWARD L. SIMMONS, currently professor and coordinator of the Higher and Postsecondary Education Program at Arizona State University, served previously as executive director of the Commission on Higher Education of the Middle States Association of Colleges and Schools. He has written and published extensively on topics related to minority issues, accreditation, community colleges, and information literacy. His research publications include *Involvement and empowerment of minorities and women in the accrediting process* and *The impact of accreditation on historically Black colleges and universities.* Dr. Simmons has been a faculty member and administrator at both two- and four-year institutions. He consults widely on a range of higher education matters, particularly on domestic and international accreditation. He earned his bachelor's degree in secondary education from Spring Hill College, a master's in Slavic languages and literature from Indiana University, and a Ph.D. in higher and postsecondary education from Florida State University.

CHANG-LIN TIEN is NEC Distinguished Professor of Engineering, a post he assumed on July 1, 1997, after seven years of service as the seventh chancellor at University of California, Berkeley—the first Asian American to head a major research university in the United States. Concurrent with his chancellorship, he was A. Martin Berlin Chair in Mechanical Engineering. A faculty member in Berkeley's Mechanical Engineering Department since 1959, he has been chair of the department (1974–81) and vice chancellor for research (1983–85). He also served as executive vice chancellor and distinguished professor at the University of California, Irvine (1988–90). Dr. Tien is internationally recognized for his scholarly contributions in the field of heat transfer. Born in Wuhan, China, and educated in Shanghai and Taiwan, where his family fled after World War II, Dr. Tien completed his undergraduate education at National Taiwan University. He came to the United States in 1956, earned a master's degree at the University of Louisville in 1957, and then a second master's and a Ph.D. at Princeton University in 1959. A recipient of many honorary doctoral degrees from universities in the United States and abroad, he currently serves on the boards of many institutions, including the Asia Foundation, Wells Fargo Bank, Raychem Corporation, Chevron Corporation, and AirTouch Communications.

ENRIQUE (HENRY) T. TRUEBA has a bachelor's degree from the Universidad Autónoma de México, a master's in philosophy from the Instituto Libre de Filosofía y Letras, a master's in theology from Woodstock College, a master's in anthropology from Stanford University, and a Ph.D. in anthropology from the University of Pittsburgh. He has edited, authored, or co-authored 19 books and has written many articles and book chapters on issues of language, culture, and education. He is a member of the Wisconsin Academy of Sciences, Arts and Letters, received the prestigious George and Louise Spindler Award in Educational Anthropology, and has occupied numerous administrative positions. He was dean of the School of Education at the University of Wisconsin, Madison, and senior vice president for Academic Affairs at the University of Houston. He is currently on leave from the University of Houston conducting research as a visiting scholar at the University of California Linguistic Minority Research Institute.

LEONARD A. VALVERDE has been in higher education for about 25 years and has served in research universities as professor, director of a research office, chair of a nationally ranked department, college dean, and academic vice president and graduate dean. Currently, he is serving as executive director of a leadership development program with a consortium of four south-western univiersities. His career goal has been to work to make quality education more accessible to underserved populations. He continues to work toward this goal, and this book contributes to his goal. He has studied, traveled, observed, and examined education in nine foreign countries. He has been called on to speak and write extensively on equal educational opportunity and cultural pluralism throughout America.

Name Index

Subject Index

References to Latinos are found under Hispanic Americans.
References to Blacks are found under African Americans.